STREET SCENE

A Play In Three Acts

By
ELMER L. RICE

SAMUEL FRENCH, INC.
45 WEST 25TH STREET   NEW YORK 10010
7623 SUNSET BOULEVARD HOLLYWOOD 90046
LONDON   TORONTO

The cast of the play as originally presented at THE PLAY-HOUSE, New York City, January 10th, 1929

WILLIAM A. BRADY, LTD.
PRESENTS

STREET SCENE

A Play in Three Acts
By ELMER RICE
DIRECTED BY THE AUTHOR
SETTING BY JO MIELZINER

CHARACTERS

(IN THE ORDER OF THEIR FIRST APPEARANCE)

ABRAHAM KAPLAN	*Leo Bulgakov*
GRETA FIORENTINO	*Eleanor Wesselhoeft*
EMMA JONES	*Beulah Bondi*
OLGA OLSEN	*Hilda Bruce*
WILLIE MAURRANT	*Russell Griffin*
ANNA MAURRANT	*Mary Servoss*
DANIEL BUCHANAN	*Conway Washburne*
FRANK MAURRANT	*Robert Kelly*
GEORGE JONES	*T. H. Manning*
STEVE SANKEY	*Joseph Baird*
AGNES CUSHING	*Jane Corcoran*
CARL OLSEN	*John M. Qualen*
SHIRLEY KAPLAN	*Anna Kostant*
FILIPPO FIORENTINO	*George Humbert*
ALICE SIMPSON	*Emily Hamill*
LAURA HILDEBRAND	*Frederica Going*
MARY HILDEBRAND	*Eileen Smith*
CHARLIE HILDEBRAND	*Alexander Lewis*
SAMUEL KAPLAN	*Horace Braham*
ROSE MAURRANT	*Erin O'Brien-Moore*
HARRY EASTER	*Glenn Coulter*
MAE JONES	*Millicent Green*
DICK McGANN	*Joseph Lee*
VINCENT JONES	*Matthew McHugh*
DR. JOHN WILSON	*John Crump*
OFFICER HARRY MURPHY	*Edward Downes*
A MILKMAN	*Ralph Willard*

A Letter-carrier..........................*Herbert Lindholm*

An Ice-man................................*Samuel S. Bonnell*

Two College Girls.......................... { *Rose Lerner* / *Astrid Alwynn* }

A Music Student.............................*Mary Emerson*

Marshall James Henry.......................*Ellsworth Jones*

Fred Cullen...............................*Jean Sidney*

An Old-clothes Man.........................*Joe Cogert*

An Interne................................*Samuel S. Bonnell*

An Ambulance Driver........................*Anthony Pawley*

A Furniture Mover...........................*Ed. A. McHugh*

Two Nurse-maids............................ { *Astrid Alwynn* / *Nelly Neil* }

Policemen................................. { *Carl C. Milter* / *John Kelly* / *Anthony Pawley* }

Two Apartment Hunters................. { *Frances F. Golden* / *Otto Frederick* }

Passers-by.........*Ruth Randolph, Elizabeth Goodyear, Josephine Coghlan, Emily Hamill, Jean Sidney, Samuel S. Bonnell, Robert Mack, John Cambridge, Carl C. Milter, Anthony Pawley, Herbert Lindholm, Ed. A. McHugh, Ralph Willard, Otto Frederick, Benn Trivers*

There is only one setting which is described in detail in the text.

The action takes place on an evening in June, and on the morning and afternoon of the following day.

STREET SCENE

ACT ONE

SCENE: The exterior of a "walk-up" apartment-house, in a mean quarter of New York. It is of ugly brownstone and was built in the '90's. Between the pavement of large, gray flagstones and the front of the house, is a deep and narrow "area-way," guarded by a rusted, ornamental iron railing. At the right, a steep flight of rotting wooden steps leads down to the cellar and to the janitor's apartment, the windows of which are just visible above the street level. Spanning the area-way is a "stoop" of four shallow, stone steps, flanked on either side by a curved stone balustrade. Beyond the broad fourth step, another step leads to the double wooden outer doors of the house; and as these are open, the vestibule, and the wide, heavy glass-panelled entrance door beyond are visible. Above the outer doors, is a glass fanlight, upon which appears the half-obliterated house number. At the left side of the doorway is a sign that reads: "Flat To-Let. 6 Rooms. Steam Heat."

On either side of the stoop, are the two narrow windows of the ground-floor apartments. In one of the windows, at the left, is a sign bearing the legend: "Prof. Filippo Fiorentino. Music for all occasions. Also instruction." Above, are the six narrow windows of the first-floor apartments, and above that, the stone sills of the second-floor windows can just be seen.

5

To the left of the house, part of the adjoining building is visible: the motor entrance to a storage warehouse. Crude boarding across the large driveway and rough planks across the sidewalk and curb indicate that an excavation is in progress. On the boarding is painted in rude lettering: "Keep Out"; and at the curb is a small barrel bearing a sign with the words: "Street Closed." To the wall of the warehouse is affixed a brass plate, bearing the name: "Patrick Mulcahy Storage Warehouse Co. Inc."

To the right of the house, scaffolding and a wooden sidewalk indicate that the house next door is being demolished. On the scaffolding is a large, wooden sign reading: "Manhattan House-Wrecking Corp."

In the close foreground, below the level of the curb, is a mere suggestion of the street.

AT RISE: The house is seen in the white glare of an arc-light, which is just off-stage to the right. The windows in the janitor's apartment are lighted, as are also those of the ground-floor apartment, at the right, and the two windows at the extreme left of the first floor. A dim, red light is affixed to the boarding of the excavation at the left.

In the lighted ground-floor window, at the right of the doorway, ABRAHAM KAPLAN is seated, in a rocking chair, reading a Yiddish newspaper. He is a Russian Jew, well past sixty: clean-shaven, thick gray hair, hooked nose, horn-rimmed spectacles. To the left of the doorway, GRETA FIORENTINO is leaning out of the window. She is forty, blonde, ruddy-faced and stout. She wears a wrapper of light, flowered material and a large pillow supports her left arm and her ample, uncorseted bosom. In her right hand is a folding paper fan, which she waves languidly.

Throughout the act and, indeed, throughout the play, there is constant noise. The noises of the city rise, fall, intermingle: the distant roar of "L" trains, automobile sirens and the whistles of boats on the river; the rattle of trucks and the indeterminate clanking of metals; fire-engines, ambulances, musical instruments, a radio, dogs barking and human voices calling, quarrelling and screaming with laughter. The noises are subdued and in the background, but they never wholly cease.

A moment after the rise of the curtain, an elderly man Enters at the right and walks into the house, exchanging a nod with MRS. FIORENTINO. A MAN, munching peanuts, crosses the stage from left to right.

A VOICE. *(offstage)* Char-lie!

(EMMA JONES appears at the left. She is middle-aged, tall and rather bony. She carries a small parcel.)

MRS. FIORENTINO. *(She speaks with a faint German accent.)* Good evening, Mrs. Jones.

MRS. JONES. *(stopping beneath MRS. FIORENTINO'S window)* Good evenin', Mrs. F. Well, I hope it's hot enough for you.

MRS. FIORENTINO. Ain't it joost awful? When I was

through with the dishes, you could take my clothes and joost wring them out.

MRS. JONES. Me, too. I ain't got a dry stitch on me.

MRS. FIORENTINO. I took off my shoes and my corset and made myself nice and comfortable, and tonight before I go to bed, I take a nice bath.

MRS. JONES. The trouble with a bath is, by the time you're all through, you're as hot as when you started.

(OLGA OLSEN, a thin, anemic Scandinavian, with untidy fair hair, comes up the cellar steps and onto the sidewalk.)

MRS. JONES. Good evenin', Mrs. Olsen. Awful hot, ain't it?

MRS. OLSEN. *(coming over to the front of the stoop)* Yust awful. Mrs. Forentiner, my hoosban' say vill you put de garbage on de doom-vaider?

MRS. FIORENTINO. Oh, sure, sure! I didn't hear him vistle. *(as MRS. JONES starts to cross to the stoop)* Don't go 'vay, Mrs. Jones. *(She disappears from the window.)*

MRS. OLSEN. *(pushing back some wisps of hair)* I tank is more cooler in de cellar.

MRS. JONES. *(sitting on the stoop and fanning herself with her parcel)* Phew! I'm just about ready to pass out.

MRS. OLSEN. My baby is crying, crying all day.

MRS. JONES. Yeah, I often say they mind the heat more'n we do. It's the same with dogs. My Queenie has jes' been layin' aroun' all day.

MRS. OLSEN. The baby get new teet'. It hurt her.

MRS. JONES. Don't tell me! If you was to know what I went t'roo with my Vincent. Half the time, he used to have convulsions.

(WILLIE MAURRANT, a disorderly boy of twelve, appears at the left, on roller skates. He stops at the left of the stoop and takes hold of the railing with both hands.)

WILLIE. *(raising his head and bawling:)* Hey, ma!

MRS. JONES. *(disapprovingly)* If you want your mother, why don't you go upstairs, instead o' yellin' like that?

WILLIE. *(Without paying the slightest attention to her, bawls louder.)* Hey, ma!

(MRS. MAURRANT appears at the one of the lighted first-floor windows. She is a fair woman of forty, who looks her age, but is by no means unattractive.)

MRS. MAURRANT. What do you want, Willie?

WILLIE. Gimme a dime, will ya? I wanna git a cone.

MRS. MAURRANT. *(to MRS. OLSEN and MRS. JONES:)* Good evening.

MRS. OLSEN and MRS. JONES. Good evenin', Mrs. Maurrant.

MRS. MAURRANT. *(to WILLIE:)* How many cones did you have today, already?

WILLIE. *(belligerently)* I'm hot! All de other guys is havin' cones. Come on, gimme a dime.

MRS. MAURRANT. Well, it's the last one. *(She disappears.)*

MRS. JONES. You certainly don't talk very nice to your mother. *(to MRS. OLSEN:)* I'd like to hear one o' mine talkin' that way to me!

MRS. MAURRANT. *(appearing at the window)* Remember, this is the last one.

WILLIE. Aw right. T'row it down.

(MRS. FIORENTINO reappears and leans out of the window again.)

MRS. MAURRANT. Catch it! *(She throws out a twist of newspaper. WILLIE scrambles for it, hastily extracts the dime, drops the newspaper on the pavement and skates off, at the left.)*

MRS. FIORENTINO. *(twisting her neck upwards)* Good evening, Mrs. Maurrant.

MRS. MAURRANT. Good evening, Mrs. Fiorentino. *(calling after WILLIE)* And don't come home too late, Willie! *(But WILLIE is already out of earshot.)*

MRS. FIORENTINO. Why don't you come down and be sociable?

MRS. MAURRANT. I'm keeping some supper warm for my husband. *(a slight pause)* Well, maybe I will for just a minute. *(She leaves the window. The lights in her apartment go out.)*

MRS. FIORENTINO. She has her troubles with dot Willie.

MRS. JONES. I guess it don't bother her much. *(significantly)* She's got her mind on other things.

MRS. OLSEN. *(looking about cautiously and coming over to the left of the stoop between the two women)* He was comin' again today to see her.

MRS. JONES. *(rising excitedly, and leaning over the balustrade)* Who — Sankey?

MRS. OLSEN. *(nodding)* Yes.

MRS. FIORENTINO. Are you sure, Mrs. Olsen?

Mrs. Olsen. I seen him. I vas doostin' de halls.

Mrs. Fiorentino. Dot's terrible!

Mrs. Jones. Wouldn't you think a woman her age, with a grown-up daughter—!

Mrs. Olsen. Two times already dis veek, I see him here.

Mrs. Jones. I seen him, meself, one day last week. He was comin' out o' the house, jest as I was comin' in wit' de dog. "Good mornin', Mrs. Jones," he says to me, as if butter wouldn't melt in his mouth. "Good mornin'," says I, lookin' him straight in the eye — *(breaking off suddenly, as the vestibule door opens)* Be careful, she's comin'.

(MRS. MAURRANT comes out of the house and stops, for a moment, on the top step.)

Mrs. Maurrant. Goodness, ain't it hot! I think it's really cooler upstairs. *(She comes down the steps to the sidewalk.)*

Mrs. Jones. Yeah, jes' what I was sayin', meself. I feel like a wet dish-rag.

Mrs. Maurrant. I would have liked to go to the Park concert tonight, if Rose had got home in time. I don't get much chance to go to concerts. My husband don't care for music. But Rose is more like me — just crazy about it.

Mrs. Jones. Ain't she home yet?

Mrs. Maurrant. No. I think maybe she had to work overtime.

Mrs. Jones. Well, all mine ever comes home for is to sleep.

MRS. FIORENTINO. The young girls nowadays—!

MRS. OLSEN. My sister was writin' me in Schweden is same t'ing—

MRS. JONES. It ain't only the young ones, either.

(A baby is heard crying in the cellar.)

OLSEN'S VOICE. *(from the cellar)* Ol-ga!

(A MAN, in a dinner jacket and straw hat, appears at the left, whistling a jazz tune. He crosses the stage and goes off at the right.)

MRS. OLSEN. *(hurrying to the right)* I betcha the baby, she's cryin' again.

OLSEN'S VOICE. Ol-ga!

MRS. OLSEN. Yes. I come right away. *(She goes down the cellar steps.)*

MRS. JONES. What them foreigners don't know about bringin' up babies would fill a book.

MRS. FIORENTINO. *(a little huffy)* Foreigners know joost as much as other people, Mrs. Jones. My mother had eight children and she brought up seven.

MRS. JONES. *(tactfully)* Well, I'm not sayin' anythin' about the Joimans. The Joimans is different — more like the Irish. What I'm talkin' about is all them squareheads an' Polacks — *(with a glance in KAPLAN'S direction)* — an' Jews.

BUCHANAN'S VOICE. *(from a third story window)* Good evening, ladies.   .

THE WOMEN. *(in unison, looking upward)* Oh, good evening, Mr. Buchanan.

BUCHANAN'S VOICE. Well, is it hot enough for you?

MRS. JONES. I'll say!

BUCHANAN'S VOICE. I was just saying to my wife, it's not the heat I mind as much as it is the humidity.

MRS. JONES. Yeah, that's it! Makes everything stick to you.

MRS. MAURRANT. How's your wife feeling in this weather?

BUCHANAN'S VOICE. She don't complain about the weather. But she's afraid to go out of the house. Thinks maybe she couldn't get back in time, in case — you know.

MRS. JONES. *(to the other women:)* I was the same way, with my Vincent — afraid to take a step. But with Mae, I was up an' out till the very last minute.

MRS. FIORENTINO. *(craning her neck upward)* Mr. Buchanan, think she would eat some nice minestrone — good Italian vegetable soup?

BUCHANAN'S VOICE. Why, much obliged, Mrs. F., but I really can't get her to eat a thing.

MRS. JONES. *(rising and looking upward)* Tell her she ought to keep up her strength. She's got two to feed, you know.

BUCHANAN'S VOICE. Excuse me, she's calling.

MRS. JONES. *(crossing to the railing, at the left of MRS. FIORENTINO)* You'd think it was him that was havin' the baby.

MRS. MAURRANT. She's such a puny little thing.

MRS. FIORENTINO. *(with a sigh)* Well, that's the way it goes. The little skinny ones have them and the big strong ones don't.

MRS. MAURRANT. Don't take it that way, Mrs. Fiorentino. You're a young woman, yet.

MRS. FIORENTINO. *(shaking her head)* Oh, well!

MRS. JONES. My aunt, Mrs. Barclay, was forty-two — *(breaking off)* Oh, good evenin', Mr. Maurrant!

(FRANK MAURRANT appears, at the left, with his coat on his arm. He is a tall, powerfully-built man of forty-five, with a rugged, grim face.)

MRS. FIORENTINO. Good evening, Mr. Maurrant.

MAURRANT. 'Evenin'. *(He goes to the stoop and seats himself, mopping his face.)* Some baby of a day!

MRS. MAURRANT. Have you been working all this while, Frank?

MAURRANT. I'll say I've been workin'. Dress-rehearsin' since twelve o'clock, with lights — in this weather. An' tomorra I gotta go to Stamford, for the try-out.

MRS. MAURRANT. Oh, you're going to Stamford tomorrow?

MAURRANT. Yeah, the whole crew's goin'. *(looking at her)* What about it?

MRS. MAURRANT. Why, nothing. Oh, I've got some cabbage and potatoes on the stove for you.

MAURRANT. I just had a plate o' beans at the Coffee Pot. All I want is a good wash. I been sweatin' like a horse, all day. *(He rises and goes up the steps.)*

MRS. FIORENTINO. My husband, too; he's sweating terrible.

MRS. JONES. Mine don't. There's some people that just naturally do, and then there's others that don't.

MAURRANT. *(to MRS. MAURRANT:)* Is anybody upstairs?

MRS. MAURRANT. No. Willie's off playing with the boys. I can't keep him home.

MAURRANT. What about Rose?

MRS. MAURRANT. I think maybe she's working overtime.

MAURRANT. I never heard o' nobody workin' nights in a real estate office.

MRS. MAURRANT. I thought maybe on account of the office being closed to-morrow — *(to the others:)* Mr. Jacobson, the head of the firm, died Tuesday, and tomorrow's the funeral, so I thought maybe—

MRS. JONES. Yeah. Leave it to the Jews not to lose a workin' day, without makin' up for it.

MAURRANT. *(to MRS. MAURRANT:)* She shouldn't be stayin' out nights without us knowin' where she is.

MRS. MAURRANT. She didn't say a word about not coming home.

MAURRANT. That's what I'm sayin', ain't it? It's a mother's place to know what her daughter's doin'.

MRS. FIORENTINO. *(soothingly)* Things are different nowadays, Mr. Maurrant, from what they used to be.

MAURRANT. Not in my family, they're not goin' to be no different. Not so long as I got somethin' to say.

A GIRL'S VOICE. *(offstage)* Red Rover! Red Rover! Let Freddie come over!

(GEORGE JONES, a short, rather plump, red-faced man, cigar in mouth, comes out of the house, as MAURRANT Enters the vestibule.)

JONES. Hello, Mr. Maurrant.

MAURRANT. *(curtly)* 'Evenin'. *(He Enters the house. JONES looks after him in surprise, for a moment. MRS. MAURRANT seats herself on the stoop.)*

JONES. Good evenin', ladies.

MRS. FIORENTINO and MRS. MAURRANT. Good evening, Mr. Jones.

JONES. *(seating himself on the left balustrade)* What's the matter with your hubby, Mrs. Maurrant? Guess he's feelin' the heat, huh?

MRS. MAURRANT. He's been working till just now and I guess he's a little tired.

MRS. JONES. Men are all alike. They're all easy to get along with so long as everythin's goin' the way they want it to . But once it don't — good night!

MRS. FIORENTINO. Yes, dot's true, Mrs. Jones.

JONES. Yeah, an' what about the women?

MRS. MAURRANT. I guess it's just the same with the women. I often think it's a shame that people don't get along better, together. People ought to be able to live together in peace and quiet, without making each other miserable.

MRS. JONES. The way I look at it, you get married for better or worse, an' if it turns out to be worse, why all you can do is make the best of it.

MRS. MAURRANT. I think the trouble is people don't make allowances. They don't realize that everybody wants a kind word, now and then. After all, we're all human, and we can't just go along by ourselves, all the time, without ever getting a kind word.

(While she is speaking, STEVE SANKEY appears, at the right. He is in the early thirties, and is prematurely bald. He is rather flashily dressed, in a patently cheap, light-gray suit, and a straw hat, with a plaid band. As he appears, MRS. JONES and MRS. FIOREN-TINO exchange a swift, significant look.)

SANKEY. *(stopping at the right of the stoop and removing his hat)* Good evening, folks! Is it hot enough for you?

THE OTHERS. Good evening.

MRS. MAURRANT. *(self-consciously)* Good evening, Mr. Sankey. *(Throughout the scene, MRS. MAURRANT and SAN-KEY try vainly to avoid looking at each other.)*

SANKEY. I don't know when we've had a day like this. Hottest June fifteenth in forty-one years. It was up to ninety-four at three p.m.

JONES. Six dead in chicago. An' no relief in sight, the evenin' paper says.

(MAURRANT appears at the window of his apartment and stands there, looking out.)

MRS. FIORENTINO. It's joost awful!

SANKEY. Well, it's good for the milk business. You know the old saying, it's an ill wind that blows nobody any good.

MRS. MAURRANT. Yes. You hardly get the milk in the morning, before it turns sour.

MRS. JONES. I'm just after pourin' half-a-bottle down the sink. *(MAURRANT leaves the window.)*

MRS. FIORENTINO. You shouldn't throw it away. You should make — what do you call it? — schmier-käs'.

SANKEY. Oh, I know what you mean — pot-cheese. My wife makes it, too, once in a while.

MRS. MAURRANT. Is your wife all right again, Mr. Sankey? You were telling me last time, she had a cold. *(MRS. JONES and MRS. FIORENTINO exchange another look.)*

SANKEY. Was I? Oh, sure, sure. That was a couple weeks ago. Yes, sure, she's all right again. That didn't amount to anything much.

MRS. JONES. You got a family, too, ain't you?

SANKEY. Yes. Yes, I have. Two little girls. Well, I got to be going along. *(He goes to the left of the stoop and stops again.)* I told my wife I'd go down to the drugstore and get her some nice cold ginger ale. You want something to cool you off in this kind of weather.

MRS. JONES. *(as SANKEY passes her)* If you ask me, all that gassy stuff don't do you a bit of good.

SANKEY. I guess you're right, at that. Still it cools you off. Well, good night, folks. See you all again. *(He strolls off, at the left, with affected nonchalance; but when he is almost out of sight, he casts a swift look back at MRS. MAURRANT.)*

(A dowdy WOMAN, wheeling a dilapidated baby carriage, appears at the left, and crosses the stage.)

JONES. What's his name — Sankey?

MRS. JONES. Yeah — Mr. Sankey.

MRS. MAURRANT. He's the collector for the milk company.

(AGNES CUSHING comes out of the house. She is a thin dried-up woman, past fifty.)

MISS CUSHING. *(coming down the steps)* Good evening.

THE OTHERS. Good evening, Miss Cushing.

MRS. MAURRANT. How is your mother today, Miss Cushing?

MISS CUSHING. *(pausing at the left of the stoop)* Why, she complains of the heat. But I'm afraid it's really her heart. She's seventy-two, you know. I'm just going down to the corner to get her a little ice-cream.

(As she goes off at the left, OLSEN, the janitor, a lanky Swede, struggles up the cellar steps with a large, covered, tin garbage-barrel. The others look around in annoyance, as be bangs the garbage barrel upon the pavement.)

OLSEN. Phew! Hot! *(He mops his face and neck with a dingy handkerchief, then lights his pipe and leans against the railing.)*

MRS. JONES. *(significantly, as she crosses to the center of the stoop and sits)* Between you and I, I don't think her mother's got long for this world. Once the heart starts goin' back on you—!

MRS. FIORENTINO. It's too bad.

MRS. MAURRANT. Poor soul! She'll have nothing at all when her mother dies. She's just spent her whole life looking after her mother.

MRS. JONES. It's no more than her duty, is it?

MRS. FIORENTINO. You could not expect that she should neglect her mother.

A VOICE. *(offstage)* Char-lie!

MRS. MAURRANT. It's not a matter of neglecting. Only — it seems as if a person should get more out of life than just looking after somebody else.

MRS. JONES. Well, I hope to tell you, after all I've done for mine, I expect 'em to look after me, in my old age.

MRS. MAURRANT. I don't know. It seems to me you might just as well not live at all, as the way she does. *(rising, with affected casualness)* I don't know what's become of Willie. I think I'd better walk down to the corner and look for him. My husband don't like it if he stays out late. *(She goes off, at the left. They all watch her, in dead silence, until she is out of earshot. Then the storm breaks.)*

MRS. JONES. *(rising excitedly)* Didja get that? Goin' to look for Willie! Can ya beat it?

MRS. FIORENTINO. It's joost terrible!

JONES. You think she's just goin' out lookin' for this guy Sankey?

MRS. JONES. *(scornfully)* Ain't men the limit? What do you think he come walkin' by here for? *(mincingly)* Just strolled by to get the wife a little ginger ale. A fat lot he cares whether his wife has ginger ale!

MRS. FIORENTINO. Two little girls he's got, too!

JONES. Yeah, that ain't right — a bird like that, wit' a wife an' two kids of his own.

MRS. FIORENTINO. The way he stands there and looks and looks at her!

MRS. JONES. An' what about the looks she was givin' him! *(seating herself again)* You'd think he was the Prince of Wales, instead of a milk collector. And didja get the crack about not seein' him for two weeks?

MRS. FIORENTINO. And joost today he was upstairs, Mrs. Olsen says.

(OLSEN approaches the stoop and removes his pipe from his mouth.)

OLSEN. *(pointing upwards)* Some day, her hoosban' is killing him. *(He replaces his pipe and goes back to his former position.)*

MRS. FIORENTINO. Dot would be terrible!

JONES. He's li'ble to, at that. You know, he's got a wicked look in his eye, dat baby has.

MRS. JONES. Well, it's no more than he deserves, the little rabbit — goin' around breakin' up people's homes. *(mockingly)* Good evenin', folks! Jes' like Whozis on the radio.

JONES. D'ya think Maurrant is wise to what's goin' on?

MRS. JONES. Well, if he ain't, there must be somethin' the matter with him. But you never can tell about men. They're as blind as bats. An' what I always say is, in a case like that, the husband or the wife is always the last one to find out.

(MISS CUSHING, carrying a small paper bag, hurries on, at the left, in a state of great excitement.)

MISS CUSHING. *(breathlessly, as she comes up the left of the stoop)* Say, what do you think! I just saw them together — the two of them!

MRS. JONES. *(rising excitedly)* What did I tell you?

MRS. FIORENTINO. Where did you see them, Miss Cushing?

MISS CUSHING. Why, right next door, in the entrance

to the warehouse. They were standing right close together. And he had his hands up on her shoulders. It's awful, isn't it?

JONES. Looks to me like this thing is gettin' pretty serious.

MRS. JONES. You didn't notice if they was kissin' or anythin', did you?

MISS CUSHING. Well, to tell you the truth, Mrs. Jones, I was so ashamed for her, that I hardly looked at all.

JONES. *(sotto voce, as the house door opens)* Look out! Maurrant's comin'.

(A conspirator's silence falls upon them, as MAURRANT, pipe in mouth, comes out of the house.)

MISS CUSHING. *(tremulously)* Good evening, Mr. Maurrant.

MAURRANT. *(on the top step)* 'Evenin'. *(to the others:)* What's become of me wife?

MRS. JONES. Why, she said she was goin' around the corner to look for Willie.

MAURRANT. *(Grunts.)* Oh.

MRS. JONES. They need a lot of lookin' after, when they're that age. *(A momentary silence)*

MISS CUSHING. Well, I think I'd better get back to my mother. *(She goes up the steps.)*

MRS. JONES & MRS. FIORENTINO & JONES. Good night, Miss Cushing.

MISS CUSHING. Good night. *(as she passes MAURRANT)* Good night, Mr. Maurrant.

MAURRANT. 'Night. *(She looks at him swiftly, and goes into the vestibule.)*

A BOY'S VOICE. *(offstage)* Red Rover! Red Rover! Let Mary come over!

(As MISS CUSHING Enters the house, SHIRLEY KAPLAN appears at the ground-floor window, at the extreme right, with a glass of steaming tea in her hand. She is a dark, unattractive Jewess, past thirty. She wears a light house dress. KAPLAN goes on reading.)

SHIRLEY. *(to the neighbors outside; she speaks with the faintest trace of accent)* Good evening.

THE OTHERS. *(not very cordially)* Good evenin'.

SHIRLEY. It's been a terrible day, hasn't it?

JONES and MRS. JONES. Yeah.

SHIRLEY. *(going to the other window)* Papa, here's your tea. Haven't you finished your paper yet? It makes it so hot, with the lights on.

KAPLAN. *(lowering his newspaper)* Oll right! Oll right! Put it out! Put it out! There is anahoo, notting to read in de papers. Notting but deevorce, skendal, and moiders. *(He speaks with a strong accent, over-emphatically and with much gesticulation. He puts his paper away, removes his glasses, and starts to drink his tea.)*

SHIRLEY. There doesn't seem to be a breath of air, anywhere. *(No one answers. SHIRLEY goes away from the window and puts out the lights.)*

MRS. JONES. *(sotto voce)* You wouldn't think anybody would want to read that Hebrew writin', would ya? I don't see how they make head or tail out of it, meself.

JONES. I guess if you learn it when you're a kid—

MRS. JONES. *(suddenly)* Well, will you look at your hubby,

Mrs. F.! He's sure got his hands full! *(She looks towards the left, greatly amused.)*

(SHIRLEY reappears at the window at the extreme right, and seats herself on the sill.)

MRS. FIORENTINO. *(leaning far out)* Joost look at him! *(calling)* Lippo, be careful you don't drop any!

LIPPO. *(offstage)* 'Allo, Margherita!

(They all watch in amusement, as FILIPPO FIORENTINO, a fat Italian, with thick black hair and moustache, comes on at the left. He is clutching a violin in his left arm and balancing five ice-cream cones in his right hand.)

LIPPO. *(shouting)* Who wantsa da ice cream cone? Nice fresha ice cream cone!

MRS. FIORENTINO. Lippo, you will drop them!

MRS. JONES. *(going up to him)* Here, gimme your violin. *(She relieves him of the violin and he shifts two of the cones to his left hand.)*

LIPPO. *(as MRS. JONES hands the violin to MRS. FIOREN- TINO)* T'ank you, Meeses Jones. 'Ere's for you a nica, fresha ice cream cone. *(MRS. FIORENTINO puts the violin on a chair behind her.)*

MRS. JONES. *(taking a cone)* Why thank you very much, Mr. F.

LIPPO. *(going up to the window)* Meeses Fiorentino, 'ere's for you a nica, fresha ice cream cone.

MRS. FIORENTINO. *(taking the cone)* It makes me too fat.

LIPPO. Ah no! Five, ten poun' more, nobody can tell da deef! *(He laughs aloud at his own joke and crosses to the stoop.)*

MRS. JONES. *(enjoying her cone)* Ain't he a sketch, though?

LIPPO. Meester Jones, you eata da cone, ha?

JONES. Why, yeah, I will at that. Thanks. Thanks.

LIPPO. Meester Maurrant?

MAURRANT. Naw; I got me pipe.

LIPPO. You lika better da pipe den da ice cream? *(crossing the stoop)* Meesa Kaplan, nice fresha cone, yes?

SHIRLEY. No, thanks. I really don't want any.

LIPPO. Meester Kaplan, yes?

KAPLAN. *(waving his hand)* No, no! Tenks, tenks!

MRS. JONES. *(to JONES:)* You oughta pay Mr. F. for the cones.

JONES. *(reluctantly reaching into his pocket)* Why, sure.

LIPPO. *(excitedly)* Ah, no, no! I don' taka da mon'. I'm treata da whole crowd. I deedn' know was gona be such a biga crowd or I bringa doz'. *(crossing to OLSEN)* Meester Olsen, you like da cone, ha?

OLSEN. Sure. Much oblige'. *(He takes the pipe from his mouth and stolidly licks the cone.)*

LIPPO. *(seating himself on the stoop, with a long sigh of relaxation)* Aaah! *(He tastes the cone and smacking his lips, looks about for approval.)* Ees tasta good, ha?

JONES. *(his mouth full)* You betcha!

MRS. JONES. It cools you off a little.

LIPPO. Sure. Dassa right. Cool you off. *(He pulls at his clothing and sits on the stoop.)* I'ma wat, wat — like I jus' come outa da bad-tub. Ees 'ota like hal in da Park. Two,

t'ree t'ousan' people, everybody sweatin' — ees smal
like menageria.

*(While he is speaking, ALICE SIMPSON, a tall, spare spinster,
appears at the right. She goes up the steps, Enters the vestibule, and
is about to push one of the buttons on the side wall.)*

MRS. JONES. *(sotto voce)* She's from the Charities. *(coming over to the stoop and calling into the vestibule)* If you're
lookin' for Mrs. Hildebrand, she ain't home yet.

MISS SIMPSON. *(coming to the doorway)* Do you know
when she'll be back?

MRS. JONES. Well, she oughta be here by now. She jus'
went around' to the Livingston. That's the pitcher-
theayter.

MISS SIMPSON. *(outraged)* You mean she's gone to a
moving picture show?

OLSEN. *(calmly)* She's comin' now.

LIPPO. *(Rising to his feet and calling vehemently)* Mees
Hil'brand! Hurry up! Hurry up! Ees a lady here. *(He
motions violently to her to hurry.)*

*(LAURA HILDEBRAND appears at the right, with her two
children, CHARLIE and MARY. She is a small, rather young
woman, with a manner of perpetual bewilderment. Both children
are chewing gum, and MARY comes on skipping a rope and chanting: "Apple, peach, pear, plum, banana." CHARLIE carefully
avoids all the cracks in the sidewalk.)*

MISS SIMPSON. *(coming out on the steps)* Well, good evening, Mrs. Hildebrand!

MRS. HILDEBRAND. *(flustered)* Good evening, Miss Simpson.

MISS SIMPSON. Where have you been? — to a moving picture show?

MRS. HILDEBRAND. Yes ma'am.

MISS SIMPSON. And where did you get the money?

MRS. HILDEBRAND. It was only seventy-five cents.

MISS SIMPSON. Seventy-five cents is a lot, when you're being dispossessed and dependent upon charity. I suppose it came out of the money I gave you to buy groceries with.

MRS. HILDEBRAND. We always went, Thursday nights, to the pictures when my husband was home.

MISS SIMPSON. Yes, but your husband isn't home. And as far as anybody knows, he has no intention of coming home.

KAPLAN. *(leaning forward out of his window)* Ees dis your conception of cherity?

SHIRLEY. Papa, why do you interfere?

MISS SIMPSON. *(to KAPLAN:)* You'll please be good enough to mind your own business.

KAPLAN. You should go home and read in your Bible de life of Christ.

MRS. JONES. *(to MRS. FIORENTINO:)* Will you listen to who's talkin' about Christ!

MISS SIMPSON. *(turning her back on KAPLAN and speaking to MRS. HILDEBRAND)* You may as well understand right now that nobody's going to give you any money to spend on moving picture shows.

LIPPO. Ah, wotsa da matter, lady? *(He thrusts his hand into his pocket and takes out a fistful of coins.)* 'Ere, you take da

mon', you go to da pitcha, ever' night. *(He forces the coins
into MRS. HILDEBRAND'S hand.)* An' here's for da bam-
bini. *(He gives each child a nickel.)*

MRS. FIORENTINO. *(to MRS. JONES:)* Dot's why we
never have money.

MRS. HILDEBRAND. *(bewildered)* I really oughtn't to
take it.

LIPPO. Sure! Sure! I got plenta mon'.

MISS SIMPSON. *(disgustedly)* We'd better go inside. I
can't talk to you here, with all these people.

MRS. HILDEBRAND. *(meekly)* Yes ma'am. *(She follows
MISS SIMPSON into the house, her children clinging to her.)*

MRS. JONES. Wouldn't she give you a pain?

LIPPO. I tella you da whola troub'. She's a don' gotta
nobody to sleepa wit'. *(The men laugh.)*

MRS. JONES. *(to MRS. FIORENTINO:)* Ain't he the
limit!

MRS. FIORENTINO. *(greatly pleased)* Tt!

LIPPO. Somebody go sleepa wit' her, she's alla right,
Meester Jones, 'ow 'bout you? *(SHIRLEY, embarrassed,
leaves the window.)*

JONES. *(with a sheepish grin)* Naw, I guess not.

LIPPO. Wot'sa matter? You 'fraid you' wife, ha? Meester
Maurrant, how 'bout you? *(MAURRANT emits a short
laugh.)*

MRS. FIORENTINO. *(delighted)* Lippo, you're joost
awful.

LIPPO. *(enjoying himself hugely)* Alla ri'. Ahma gonna go
myself! *(He laughs boisterously. The others laugh too.)*

MRS. JONES. *(suddenly)* Here's your wife, now, Mr.
Maurrant.

(A sudden silence falls upon them all, as MRS. MAURRANT approaches at the left. A swift glance apprises her of MAURRANT'S presence.)

LIPPO. 'Allo, Meeses Maurrant. Why you don' come to da concerto?

MRS. MAURRANT. Well, I was waiting for Rose, but she didn't get home. *(to MAURRANT: as she starts to go up the steps)* Is she home yet, Frank?

MAURRANT. No, she ain't. Where you been all this while?

MRS. MAURRANT. Why, I've been out looking for Willie.

MAURRANT. I'll give him a good fannin', when I get hold of him.

MRS. MAURRANT. Ah, don't whip him, Frank, please don't. All boys are wild like that, when they're that age.

JONES. Sure! My boy Vincent was the same way. An' look at him, today — drivin' his own taxi an' makin' a good livin'.

LIPPO. *(leaning on the balustrade)* Ees jussa same t'ing wit' me. W'en Ahm twelva year, I run away — I don' never see my parent again.

MAURRANT. That's all right about that. But it ain't gonna be that way in my family.

MRS. MAURRANT. *(as MISS SIMPSON comes out of the house)* Look out, Frank. Let the lady pass.

MISS SIMPSON. Excuse me. *(They make way for her, as she comes down the steps. MRS. MAURRANT seats herself on the stoop.)*

LIPPO. Meeses Hil'brand, she gotta de tougha luck, ha? Tomorra, dey gonna t'row 'er out in da street, ha?

MISS SIMPSON. *(stopping at the right of the stoop and turning towards him)* Yes, they are. And if she has any place to sleep, it will only be because the Charities find her a place. And you'd be doing her a much more neighborly act, if you helped her to realize the value of money, instead of encouraging her to throw it away.

LIPPO. *(with a deprecatory shrug)* Ah, lady, no! I give 'er coupla dollar, make 'er feel good, maka me feel good — dat don' 'urt nobody. *(SHIRLEY reappears at the window.)*

MISS SIMPSON. Yes it does. It's bad for her character.

KAPLAN. *(throwing away his cigarette and laughing aloud)* Ha! You mek me leff!

MISS SIMPSON. *(turning, angrily)* Nobody's asking your opinion.

KAPLAN. Dot's oll right. I'm taling you wit'out esking. You hoid maybe already dot poem:
"Orgenized cherity, measured and iced,
    In der name of a kushus, stetistical Christ."

MISS SIMPSON. *(fiercely)* All the same, you Jews are the first to run to the Charities. *(She strides angrily off at the right. LIPPO, affecting a mincing gait, pretends to follow her.)*

KAPLAN. *(leaning out of the window)* Come back and I'll tal you somet'ing will maybe do good your kerecter.

MRS. FIORENTINO. Lippo!

MRS. JONES. *(highly amused)* Look at him, will ya?

LIPPO. *(laughing and waving his hand)* Gooda-bye, lady! *(He comes back to the stoop.)*

KAPLAN. *(to the others:)* Dey toin out in de street a mudder vit' two children, and dis female comes and preaches to her bourgeois morelity.

MRS. JONES. *(to MRS. FIORENTINO:)* He's shootin' off his face again.

SHIRLEY. Papa, it's time to go to bed!

KAPLAN. *(irritably)* Lat me alone, Shoiley. *(rising and addressing the others)* Dees cherities are notting but anudder dewise for popperizing de verking klesses. W'en de lendlords steal from de verkers a million dollars, dey give to de Cherities a t'ousand.

MAURRANT. Yeah? Well, who's puttin' her out on the street? What about the lan'lord here? He's a Jew, ain't he?

MRS. JONES. I'll say he's a Jew! Isaac Cohen!

KAPLAN. Jews oder not Jews — wot has dis got to do vit' de quastion? I'm not toking releegion, I'm toking economics. So long as de kepitalist klesses—

MAURRANT. *(interrupting)* I'm talkin' about if you don't pay your rent, you gotta move.

MRS. MAURRANT. It doesn't seem right, though, to put a poor woman out of her home.

MRS. FIORENTINO. And for her husband to run away — dot vos not right either.

LIPPO. I betcha 'e's got 'nudder woman. He find a nice blonda chicken, 'e run away.

MRS. JONES. There ought to be a law against women goin' around, stealin' other women's husbands.

MRS. FIORENTINO. Yes, dot's right, Mrs. Jones.

MAURRANT. Well, what I'm sayin' is, it ain't the landlord's fault.

KAPLAN. Eet's de folt of our economic system. So long as de institution of priwate property exeests, de verkers will be at de moicy of de property owning klesses.

MAURRANT. That's a lot o' bushwa! I'm a woikin' man see? I been payin' dues for twenty-two years in the Stage Hands Union. If we're not gettin' what we want, we call a strike, see? — and then we get it.

LIPPO. Sure! Ees same wit' me. We gotta Musician Union. We getta pay for da rehears', we getta pay for da overtime—

SHIRLEY. That's all right when you belong to a strong union. But when a union is weak, like the Teacher's Union, it doesn't do you any good.

MRS. JONES. (to MRS. FIORENTINO:) Can y' imagine that? — teachers belongin' to a union!

KAPLAN. (impatiently) Oll dese unions eccomplish notting wotever. Oll dis does not toch de fondamental problem. So long as de tuls of industry are in de hands of de kepitalist klesses, ve vill hev exploitation and sloms and—

MAURRANT. T' hell wit' all dat hooey! I'm makin' a good livin' an' I'm not doin' any kickin'.

OLSEN. (removing his pipe from his mouth) Ve got prosperity, dis coontry.

JONES. You said somethin'!

KAPLAN. Sure, for de reech is planty prosperity! Mister Morgan rides in his yacht and upstairs de toin a voman vit' two children in de street.

MAURRANT. And if you was to elect a Socialist president tomorra, it would be the same thing.

MRS. FIORENTINO. Yes, dot's right, Mr. Maurrant.

JONES. You're right!

KAPLAN. Who's toking about electing presidents? Ve must put de tuls of industry in de hends of de vorking klesses and dis ken be accomplished only by a sushal revolution!

MAURRANT. Yeah? Well, we don't want no revolutions in this country, see? *(general chorus of assent)*

MRS. JONES. I know all about that stuff — teachin' kids there ain't no Gawd an' that their gran'fathers was monkeys.

JONES. *(rising, angrily)* Free love, like they got in Russia, huh? *(KAPLAN makes a gesture of impatient disgust, and sinks back into his chair.)*

MAURRANT. There's too goddam many o' you Bolshevikis runnin' aroun' loose. If you don't like the way things is run here, why in hell don't you go back where you came from?

SHIRLEY. Everybody has a right to his own opinion, Mr. Maurrant.

MAURRANT. Not if they're against law and order, they ain't. We don't want no foreigners comin' in, tellin' us how to run things.

MRS. FIORENTINO. It's nothing wrong to be a foreigner. Many good people are foreigners.

LIPPO. Sure! Looka Eetalians. Looka Cristoforo Colombo! 'E'sa firs' man discov' America — 'e's Eetalian, jussa like me.

MAURRANT. I'm not sayin' anythin' about that—

OLSEN. *(removing his pipe)* Firs' man is Lief Ericson.

LIPPO. *(excitedly, going towards Olsen)* Wassa dat?

OLSEN. Firs' man is Lief Ericson.

LIPPO. No! No! Colombo! Cristoforo Colomb' — 'e'sa firs' man discov' America — ever'body knowa dat! *(He looks about appealingly.)*

MRS. JONES. Why, sure, everybody knows that.

JONES. Every kid learns that in school.

SHIRLEY. Ericson was really the first discoverer—

LIPPO. *(yelling)* No! Colomb!

SHIRLEY. But Columbus was the first to open America to settlement.

LIPPO. *(happily, as he goes back to the stoop)* Sure, dassa wot Ahm say — Colomb' is firs'.

OLSEN. Firs' man is Lief Ericson. *(LIPPO taps his forehead, significantly.)*

LIPPO. Looka wot Eetalian do for America — 'e build bridge, 'e build railroad, 'e build subway, 'e dig sewer. Wit' out Eetalian, ees no America.

JONES. Like I heard a feller sayin': the Eye-talians built New York, the Irish run it an' the Jews own it. *(laughter)*

MRS. FIORENTINO. *(convulsed)* Oh! Dot's funny!

JONES. *(pleased with his success)* Yep; the Jews own it all right.

MAURRANT. Yeah, an' they're the ones that's doin' all the kickin'.

SHIRLEY. It's no disgrace to be a Jew, Mr. Maurrant.

MAURRANT. I'm not sayin' it is. All I'm sayin' is, what we need in this country is a little more respect for law an' order. Look at what's happenin' to people's homes, with all this divorce an' one thing an' another. Young girls goin' around smokin' cigarettes an' their skirts up around their necks. An' a lot o' long haired guys talkin' about free love an' birth control an' breakin' up decent people's homes. I tell you it's time somethin' was done to put the fear o' God into people!

MRS. JONES. Good for you, Mr. Maurrant!

JONES. You're damn right.

MRS. FIORENTINO. Dot's right, Mr. Maurrant!

MRS. MAURRANT. Sometimes, I think maybe they're only trying to get something out of life.

MAURRANT. Get somethin', huh? Somethin' they oughtn't to have, is that it?

MRS. MAURRANT. No; I was only thinking—

MAURRANT. Yeah, you were only thinkin', huh?

KAPLAN. *(rising to his feet again)* De femily is primerily an economic institution.

MRS. JONES. *(to MRS. FIORENTINO:)* He's in again.

KAPLAN. W'en priwate property is ebolished, de femily will no longer hev eny reason to exeest.

SHIRLEY. Can't you keep quiet, papa?

MAURRANT. *(belligerently)* Yeah? Is that so? No reason to exist, huh? Well, it's gonna exist, see? Children respectin' their parents an' doin' what they're told, get me? An' husbands an' wives, lovin' an' honorin' each other, like they said they would, when they was spliced — an' any dirty sheeny that says different is li'able to get his head busted open, see?

MRS. MAURRANT. *(springing to her feet)* Frank!

SHIRLEY. *(trying to restrain KAPLAN)* Papa!

KAPLAN. Oll right! I should argue vit' a low kless gengster.

MAURRANT. *(raging)* Who's a gangster? Why, you goddam—! *(He makes for the balustrade.)*

MRS. MAURRANT. *(seizing his arm)* Frank!

JONES. *(seizing the other arm)* Hey! Wait a minute! Wait a minute!

MAURRANT. Lemme go!

SHIRLEY. *(interposing herself)* You should be ashamed to talk like that to an old man! *(She slams down the window.)*

MAURRANT. Yeah? *(to MRS. MAURRANT and JONES)* All right, lemme go! I ain't gonna do nothin'. *(They release him. SHIRLEY expostulates with KAPLAN and leads him away from the window.)*

MRS. JONES. *(who has run over to the right of the stoop)* Maybe if somebody handed him one, he'd shut up with his talk for a while.

LIPPO. 'E talka lika dat een Eetaly, Mussolini's gonna geeve 'eem da castor-oil.

MRS. JONES. *(laughing)* Yeah? Say, that's a funny idea! *(Still chuckling, she goes back to the railing at the left of the stoop.)*

JONES. No kiddin', is that what they do?

MRS. FIORENTINO. Yes, dot's true. My husband read it to me in the Italian paper.

MRS. MAURRANT. Why must people always be hurting and injuring each other? Why can't they live together in peace?

MAURRANT. *(mockingly)* Live in peace! You're always talkin' about livin' in peace!

MRS. MAURRANT. Well, it's true, Frank. Why can't people just as well be kind to each other?

MAURRANT. Then let 'im go live with his own kind.

JONES. *(coming down the steps)* Yeah, that's what I say. *(as*

MRS. JONES laughs aloud) What's eatin' you?

MRS. JONES. I was just thinkin' about the castor-oil. *(MAURRANT seats himself on the right balustrade.)*

LIPPO. Sure, 'esa funny fell', Mussolini. *(doubling up in mock pain)* 'E geeve 'em da pain in da belly, dey no can talk. *(suddenly)* Look! 'Eresa da boy. 'Esa walk along da street an' reada da book. Datsa da whola troub': reada too much book.

(While LIPPO is speaking, SAMUEL KAPLAN appears at the left. He is twenty-one, slender, with dark, unruly hair and a sensitive, mobile face. He is hatless, and his coat is slung over one shoulder. He walks along slowly, absorbed in a book. As he approaches the stoop, SHIRLEY, in a kimono, appears at the closed window, opens it, and is about to go away again, when she sees SAM.)

SHIRLEY. *(calling)* Sam!

SAM. *(looking up)* Hello, Shirley.

SHIRLEY. Are you coming in?

SAM. No, not yet. It's too hot to go to bed.

SHIRLEY. Well, I'm tired. And papa's going to bed, too. So don't make a noise when you come in.

SAM. I won't.

SHIRLEY. Good night.

SAM. Good night. *(SHIRLEY goes away from the window. To the others, as he seats himself on the curb to the right of the stoop.)* Good evening!

SEVERAL. 'Evening.

LIPPO. *(approaching SAM)* 'Ow you lika da concerto? I see you sittin' in da fronta seat.

SAM. I didn't like it. Why don't they play some real music, instead of all those Italian organ-grinder's tunes?

LIPPO. *(excitedly)* Wotsa da matter? You don't lika da Verdi?

SAM. No, I don't. It's not music!

LIPPO. Wot you call music — da Tschaikov's ha? *(He hums derisively a few bars from the first movement of the Symphonie Pathetique.)*

SAM. Yes, Tschaikovsky — and Beethoven. Music that comes from the soul.

MRS. MAURRANT. The one I like is— *(She hums the opening bars of Mendelssohn's Spring Song.)*

LIPPO. Dotsa da Spreeng Song from da Mendelson.

MRS. MAURRANT. Yes! I love that. *(She goes on humming softly.)*

MRS. FIORENTINO. And the walzer von Johann Strauss. *(She hums the Wienerwald Waltz.)*

MRS. JONES. Well, gimme a good jazz band, every time.

LIPPO. *(protesting)* Ah no! Ees not music, da jazz. Ees breaka your ear. *(He imitates the discordant blaring of a saxophone.)*

JONES. *(bored)* Well, I guess I'll be on me way.

MRS. JONES. Where are *you* goin'?

JONES. Just around to Callahan's to shoot a little pool. Are you comin' along, Mr. Maurrant?

MAURRANT. I'm gonna wait awhile.

(A man, with a clubfoot, appears at the right and crosses the stage.)

MRS. JONES. *(as JONES goes toward the right)* Don't be comin' home lit, at all hours o' the mornin'.

JONES. *(over his shoulder)* Aw, lay off dat stuff! I'll be back in a half-an-hour. *(He goes off, at the right.)*

A VOICE. *(offstage)* Char-lie!

MRS. JONES. Him an' his pool! Tomorra he won't be fit to go to work, again.

SAM. *(who has been awaiting a chance to interrupt)* When you hear Beethoven, it expresses the struggles and emotions of the human soul.

LIPPO. *(waving him aside)* Ah, ees no good, da Beethoven. Ees alla time sad, sad. Ees wanna maka you cry. I don' wanna cry, I wanna laugh. Eetalian music ees make you 'appy. Ees make you feel good. *(He sings several bars of Donna è mobile.)*

MRS. MAURRANT. *(applauding)* Yes, I like that, too.

LIPPO. Ah, ees bew-tiful! Ees maka you feela fine. Ees maka you wanna dance. *(He executes several dance steps.)*

MRS. FIORENTINO. *(rising)* Vait, Lippo, I vill give you music. *(She goes away from the window. The lights go on, in the Fiorentino apartment.)*

LIPPO. *(calling after her)* Playa Puccini, Margherita! *(He hums an air from Madame Butterfly. Then as MRS. FIOREN-TINO begins to play the waltz from La Bohême on the paino.)* Ah! La Bohême! Bew-tiful! Who'sa gonna dance wit' me? Meeses Maurrant, 'ow 'bout you?

MRS. MAURRANT. *(with an embarrassed laugh)* Well, I don't know. *(She looks timidly at MAURRANT, who gives no sign.)*

LIPPO. Ah, come on! Dansa wit' me! *(He takes her by the hand.)*

MRS. MAURRANT. Well, all right, I will.

LIPPO. Sure, we hava nica dance. *(They begin to dance on the sidewalk. To MAURRANT:)* Your wife ees dansa swell.

MRS. MAURRANT. *(laughing)* Oh, go on, Mr. Fiorentino! But I always loved to dance!

(They dance on. SANKEY appears, at the left, carrying a paper-bag, from which the neck of a ginger ale bottle protrudes. MAURRANT sees him and rises.)

MRS. JONES. *(following MAURRANT'S stare and seeing SANKEY)* Look out! You're blockin' traffic!

SANKEY. *(stopping at the left of the stoop)* I see you're having a little dance. *(MRS. MAURRANT sees him and stops dancing. LIPPO leans against the right balustrade, panting. The music goes on.)* Say, go right ahead. Don't let me stop you.

MRS. MAURRANT. Oh, that's all right. I guess we've danced about enough. *(She goes up the steps, ill at ease.)*

SANKEY. It's a pretty hot night for dancing.

MRS. MAURRANT. Yes, it is.

SANKEY. *(going towards the right)* Well, I got to be going along. Good night, folks.

THE OTHERS. *(except MAURRANT)* Good night.

LIPPO. *(as he seats himself at the left of the stoop)* Stoppa da music, Margherita! *(The music stops. SANKEY goes off, at the right. MRS. MAURRANT goes quickly up the steps.)*

MAURRANT. *(stopping her)* Who's that bird?

MRS. MAURRANT. Why, that's Mr. Sankey. He's the milk collector.

MAURRANT. Oh, he is, is he? Well, what's he hangin' around here for?

MRS. MAURRANT. Well, he lives just down the block, somewhere.

MRS. JONES. He's just been down to the drug store, gettin' some ginger ale for his wife.

MAURRANT. Yeah? Well, what I want to know is, why ain't Rose home yet?

MRS. MAURRANT. I told you, Frank—

MAURRANT. I know all about what you told me. What I'm sayin' is, you oughta be lookin' after your kids, instead of doin' so much dancin'.

MRS. MAURRANT. Why, it's the first time I've danced, in I don't know when.

MAURRANT. That's all right, about that. But I want 'em home, instead o' battin' around the streets, hear me?

(While he is speaking, WILLIE appears sobbing, at the left, his clothes torn and his face scratched. He is carrying his skates.)

MRS. MAURRANT. *(coming down the steps)* Why, Willie, what's the matter? *(reproachfully, as WILLIE comes up to her, sniffling)* Have you been fighting again?

WILLIE. *(with a burst of indignation)* Well, dat big bum ain't gonna say dat to me. I'll knock da stuffin's out o' him, dat's what I'll do!

MAURRANT. *(tensely, as he comes down the steps)* Who's been sayin' things to you?

WILLIE. Dat big bum, Joe Connolly, dat's who! *(blubbering)* I'll knock his goddam eye out, next time!

MRS. MAURRANT. Willie!

MAURRANT. *(seizing WILLIE'S arm)* Shut up your swearin', do you hear? — or I'll give you somethin' to bawl for. What did he say to you, huh? What did he say to you?

WILLIE. *(struggling)* Ow! Leggo my arm!

MRS. MAURRANT. What difference does it make what a little streetloafer like that says?

MAURRANT. Nobody's askin' you! *(to WILLIE:)* What did he say? *(He and MRS. MAURRANT exchange a swift involuntary look; then MAURRANT releases the boy.)* G'wan up to bed now, an' don't let me hear no more out o' you. *(raising his hand)* G'wan now. Beat it! *(WILLIE ducks past MAURRANT and hurries up the steps and into the vestibule.)*

MRS. MAURRANT. Wait, Willie, I'll go with you. *(She goes up the steps, then stops and turns.)* Are you coming up, Frank?

MAURRANT. No I ain't. I'm goin' around to Callahan's for a drink, an' if Rose ain't home, when I get back, there's gonna be trouble. *(Without another glance or word, he goes off at the right. MRS. MAURRANT looks after him for a moment, with a troubled expression.)*

MRS. MAURRANT. *(Entering the vestibule)* Well, good night, all.

THE OTHERS. Good night. *(SAM rises. MRS. MAURRANT and WILLIE Enter the house.)*

(MRS. FIORENTINO reappears at the window.)

MRS. FIORENTINO. Lippo! *(She sees that something is wrong.)*

MRS. JONES. Say, you missed it all! *(SAM, about to go up the steps, stops at the right of the stoop.)*

MRS. FIORENTINO. *(eagerly)* Vat?

MRS. JONES. *(volubly)* Well, they was dancin', see? An' who should come along but Sankey!

MRS. FIORENTINO. Tt!

(A light appears in the Maurrant apartment.)

MRS. JONES. Well, there was the three o' them — Mr. Maurrant lookin' at Sankey as if he was ready to kill him, an' Mrs. Maurrant as white as a sheet, an' Sankey, as innocent as the babe unborn.

MRS. FIORENTINO. Did he say something

MRS. JONES. No, not till after Sankey was gone. Then he wanted to know who he was an' what he was doin' here. "He's the milk collector," she says.

MRS. FIORENTINO. It's joost awful.

MRS. JONES. Oh, an' then Willie comes home.

LIPPO. Da boy tella 'eem 'is mamma ees a whore an' Weelie leeck 'im.

MRS. JONES. Well, an' what else is she?

SAM. *(unable longer to restrain himself)* Stop it! Stop it! Can't you let her alone? Have you no hearts? Why do you tear her to pieces, like a pack of wolves? It's cruel, cruel! *(He chokes back a sob, then dashes abruptly into the house.)*

LIPPO. *(rising to his feet and yelling after him)* Wotsa matter you?

MRS. JONES. Well, listen to him, will you! He must be goin' off his nut, too.

LIPPO. 'Esa reada too mucha book. Ees bad for you.

MRS. FIORENTINO. I think he is loving the girl.

MRS. JONES. Yeah? Well, that's all the Maurrants need

is to have their daughter get hooked up wit' a Jew. It's a fine house to be livin' in, ain't it, between the Maurrants upstairs, an' that bunch o' crazy Jews down here.

(A girl appears at the left, glancing apprehensively, over her shoulder, at a man who is walking down the street behind her. They cross the stage and go off, at the right. MRS. JONES speaks as MRS. OLSEN comes up the cellar steps and over to the stoop.)

MRS. JONES. Well, good night.

MRS. FIORENTINO. Good night, Mrs. Jones.

LIPPO. Goo' night, Meeses Jones.

MRS. JONES. Wait a minute, Mrs. Olsen. I'll go with you. *(MRS. JONES and MRS. OLSEN Enter the house. OLSEN yawns mightly, knocks the ashes from his pipe, and goes down the cellar steps. WILLIE MAURRANT leans out of the window and spits into the area way. Then he leaves the window and turns out the light.)*

(A Policeman appears, at the right, and strolls across the stage.)

LIPPO. *(who has gone up the steps)* Margherita, eef I ever ketcha you sleepin' wit' da meelkaman, Ahm gonna breaka your neck.

MRS. FIORENTINO. *(yawning)* Stop your foolishness, Lippo, and come to bed! *(LIPPO laughs and Enters the house. MRS. FIORENTINO takes the pillow off the window-sill, closes the window, and starts to pull down the shade.)*

(ROSE MAURRANT and HARRY EASTER appear at the left.

ROSE is a pretty girl of twenty, cheaply but rather tastefully dressed. EASTER is about thirty-five, good looking, and obviously prosperous.)

MRS. FIORENTINO. Good evening, Miss Maurrant.

ROSE. *(as they pass the window)* Oh, good evening, Mrs. Fiorentino. *(ROSE and EASTER cross to the stoop. MRS. FIORENTINO looks at them a moment, then pulls down the shade and turns out the lights.)*

ROSE. *(stopping at the foot of the steps)* Well, this is where I live, Mr. Easter. *(She extends her hand.)* I've had a lovely time.

EASTER. *(taking her hand)* Why, you're not going to leave me like this, are you? I've hardly had a chance to talk to you.

ROSE. *(laughing)* We've been doing nothing but talking since six o'clock. *(She tries gently to extricate her hand.)*

EASTER. *(still holding it)* No, we haven't. We've been eating and dancing. And now, just when I want to talk to you — *(He puts his other arm around her.)* Rose—

ROSE. *(rather nervously)* Please don't, Mr. Easter. Please let go. I think there's somebody coming.

(She frees herself, as the house door opens and MRS. OLSEN appears in the vestibule. They stand in silence, as MRS. OLSEN puts the door off the latch, tries it to see that it is locked, dims the light in the vestibule and comes out on the stoop.)

MRS. OLSEN. *(as she comes down the steps)* Goot evening, Miss Maurrant. *(She darts a swift look at EASTER and crosses to the cellar steps.)*

ROSE. Good evening, Mrs. Olsen. How's the baby?

MRS. OLSEN. She vas cryin' all the time. I tank she vas gettin' new teet'.

ROSE. Oh, the poor little thing! What a shame!

MRS. OLSEN. *(as she goes down the steps)* Yes, ma'am. Goot night, Miss Maurrant.

ROSE. Good night, Mrs. Olsen. *(to EASTER:)* She's got the cutest little baby you ever saw.

EASTER. *(rather peevishly)* Yeah? That's great. *(taking ROSE'S hand again)* Rose, listen—

ROSE. I've really got to go upstairs now, Mr. Easter. It's awfully late.

EASTER. Well, can't I come up with you, for a minute?

ROSE. *(positively)* No, of course not!

EASTER. Why not?

ROSE. Why, we'd wake everybody up. Anyhow, my father wouldn't like it.

EASTER. Aren't you old enough to do what you like?

ROSE. It's not that. Only I think when you're living with people, there's no use doing things you know they don't like. *(embarrassed)* Anyhow, there's only the front room and my little brother sleeps there. So good night, Mr. Easter.

EASTER. *(taking both her hands)* Rose — I'm crazy about you.

ROSE. Please let me go, now.

EASTER. Kiss me good-night.

ROSE. No.

EASTER. Why not, hm?

ROSE. I don't want to.

EASTER. Just one kiss.

ROSE. No.

EASTER. Yes! *(He takes her in his arms and kisses her. ROSE frees herself and goes to the right of the stoop.)*

ROSE. *(Her bosom heaving.)* It wasn't nice of you to do that.

EASTER. *(going over to her)* Why not? Didn't you like it? Hm?

ROSE. Oh, it's not that.

EASTER. Then what is it, hm?

ROSE. *(turning and facing him)* You know very well what it is. You've got a wife, haven't you?

EASTER. What of it? I tell you I'm clean off my nut about you.

ROSE. *(nervously, as the house door opens)* Look out! Somebody's coming. *(EASTER goes to the other side of the stoop and they fall into a self-conscious silence.)*

(MRS. JONES comes out of the house, leading an ill-conditioned dog.)

MRS. JONES. *(as she comes down the steps)* Oh, good evenin'. *(She stares at EASTER, then goes towards the right.)*

ROSE. Good evening, Mrs. Jones. It's been a terrible day, hasn't it.

MRS. JONES. Yeah. Awful. *(stopping)* I think your father's been kinda worried about you.

ROSE. Oh, has he?

MRS. JONES. Yeah. Well, I gotta give Queenie her exercise. Good night. *(She stares at EASTER again, then goes off at right.)*

Rose. Good night, Mrs. Jones. *(to EASTER:)* I'll soon have all the neighbors talking about me.

Easter. *(going over to her again)* What can they say, hm? — that they saw you saying good night to somebody on the front door step?

Rose. They can say worse than that — and what's more, they will, too.

Easter. Well, why not snap out of it all?

Rose. Out of what?

Easter. *(indicating the house)* This! The whole business. Living in a dirty old tenement like this; working all day in a real estate office, for a measly twenty-five a week. You're not going to try to tell me you like living this way, are you?

Rose. No, I can't say that I like it, especially. But maybe it won't always be this way. Anyhow, I guess I'm not so much better than anybody else.

Easter. *(taking her hand)* Do you know what's the matter with you? You're not wise to yourself. Why, you've got just about everything, you have. You've got looks and personality and a bean on your shoulders — there's nothing you haven't got. You've got it, I tell you.

Rose. You shouldn't keep looking at me, all the time, at the office. The other girls are beginning to pass hints about it.

Easter. *(releasing her hand, genuinely perturbed)* Is that a fact? You see, that shows you! I never even knew I was looking at you. I guess I just can't keep my eyes off you. Well, we've got to do something about it.

Rose. *(nervously snapping the clasp of her handbag)* I guess the only thing for me to do is to look for another job.

EASTER. Yes, that's what I've been thinking, too. *(as she is about to demur)* Wait a minute, honey! I've been doing a little thinking and I've got it all doped out. The first thing you do is throw up your job, see?

ROSE. But—

EASTER. Then you find yourself a nice, cozy little apartment somewhere. *(as she is about to interrupt again)* Just a minute, now! Then you get yourself a job on the stage.

ROSE. How could I get a job on the stage?

EASTER. Why, as easy as walking around the block. I've got three or four friends in the show business. Ever hear of Harry Porkins?

ROSE. No.

EASTER. Well, he's the boy that put on Mademoiselle Marie last year. He's an old pal of mine, and all I'd have to say to him is: *(putting his arm around her shoulder)* "Harry, here's a little girl I'm interested in," and he'd sign you up in a minute.

ROSE. I don't think I'd be any good on the stage.

EASTER. Why, what are you talking about, sweetheart? There's a dozen girls, right now, with their names up in electric lights, that haven't got half your stuff. All you got to do is go about it in the right way — put up a little front, see? Why, half the game is nothing but bluff. Get yourself a classy little apartment, and fill it up with trick furniture, see? Then you doll yourself up in a flock of Paris clothes and you throw a couple or three parties and you're all set. *(taking her arm)* Wouldn't you *like* to be on Broadway?

ROSE. I don't believe I ever could be.

EASTER. Isn't it worth trying? What have you got here, hm? This is no kind of a racket for a girl like you. *(taking her hand)* You do like me a little, don't you?

ROSE. I don't know if I do or not.

EASTER. Why, sure you do. and once you get to know me better, you'd like me even more. I'm no Valentino, but I'm not a bad scout. Why, think of all the good times we could have together — you with a little apartment and all. And maybe we could get us a little car—

ROSE. And what about your wife?

EASTER. *(letting go her hand)* The way I figure it is, she doesn't have to know anything about it. She stays up there in Bronxville, and there are lots of times when business keeps me in New York. Then, in the summer, she goes to the mountains. Matter of fact, she's going next week and won't be back until September.

ROSE. *(shaking her head and going towards the stoop)* I don't think it's the way I'd want things to be.

EASTER. Why, there's nothing really wrong about it.

ROSE. Maybe there isn't. But it's just the way I feel about it, I guess.

EASTER. Why, you'd get over that in no time. There's lots of girls—

ROSE. Yes, I know there are. But you've been telling me all along I'm different.

EASTER. Sure, you're different. You're in a class by yourself. Why, sweetheart — *(He tries to take her in his arms.)*

ROSE. *(pushing him away)* No. And you mustn't call me sweetheart.

EASTER. Why not?

Rose. Because I'm not your sweetheart.

Easter. I want you to be—

(A sudden yell of pain is heard from upstairs. They both look up, greatly startled.)

Easter. My God, what's that — a murder?

Rose. It must be poor Mrs. Buchanan. She's expecting a baby.

Easter. Why does she yell like that? God, I thought somebody was being killed.

Rose. The poor thing! *(with sudden impatience, she starts up the steps)* I've got to go, now. Good night.

Easter. *(taking her hand)* But, Rose—

Rose. *(freeing her hand quickly)* No, I've got to go. *(suddenly)* Look, there's my father. There'll only be an argument, if he sees you.

Easter. All right, I'll go.

(He goes through the left, as MAURRANT appears at the right.)

Rose. *(going up to the top step)* Good night.

Easter. Good night. *(He goes off, at the left. ROSE begins searching in her hand bag for her latch key.)*

Rose. *(as MAURRANT approaches)* Hello, pop.

Maurrant. *(stopping at the foot of the steps)* Who was that you was talkin' to?

Rose. That's Mr. Easter. He's the manager of the office.

Maurrant. what's he doin' here? You been out wit' him?

Rose. Yes, he took me out to dinner.

Maurrant. Oh, he did, huh?

Rose. Yes, I had to stay late to get out some letters. You see, pop, the office is closed tomorrow, on account of Mr. Jacobson's funeral—

Maurrant. Yeah, I know all about that. This is a hell of a time to be gettin' home from dinner.

Rose. Well, we danced afterwards.

Maurrant. Oh, you danced, huh? With a little pettin' on the side, is that it?

Rose. *(rather angrily, as she seats herself on the left balustrade)* I don't see why you can never talk to me in a nice way.

Maurrant. So you're startin' to go on pettin' parties, are you?

Rose. Who said I was on a petting party?

Maurrant. I suppose he didn't kiss you or nothin', huh?

Rose. No, he didn't! and if he did—

Maurrant. It's your own business, is that it? *(going up the steps)* Well, I'm gonna make it my business, see? Is this bird married? *(ROSE does not answer.)* I t'ought so! They're all alike, them guys — all after the one thing. Well, get this straight. No married men ain't gonna come nosin' around my family, get me?

Rose. *(rising agitatedly, as the house door opens)* Be quiet, pop! There's somebody coming.

Maurrant. I don't care!

(BUCHANAN hurries out of the house. He is a small and pasty young man — a typical, "white collar slave." He has hastily put on

his coat and trousers over his pajamas and his bare feet are in slippers.)

BUCHANAN. *(as he comes down the steps)* I think the baby's coming!

ROSE. *(solicitously)* Can I do anything, Mr. Buchanan?

BUCHANAN. *(as he hurries towards the left)* No, I'm just going to phone for the doctor.

ROSE. *(coming down the steps)* Let me do it, and you go back to your wife.

BUCHANAN. Well, if your wouldn't mind. It's Doctor John Wilson. *(handing her a slip of paper)* Here's his number. And the other number is her sister, Mrs. Thomas. And here's two nickels. Tell them both to come right away. She's got terrible pains.

(Another scream from upstairs.)

BUCHANAN. Listen to her! I better go back. *(He dashes up the steps and into the house.)*

ROSE. Oh, the poor woman! Pop, tell ma to go up to her. Hurry!

MAURRANT. Aw, all right. He follows BUCHANAN into the house. ROSE hurries off at the left.)

(MAE JONES and DICK McGann appear. MAE is a vulgar shop-girl of twenty-one; DICK, a vacuous youth of about the same age. MAE is wearing DICK'S straw hat and they are both quite drunk.)

MAE. *(to ROSE:)* Hello, Rose. What's your hurry?

Rose. *(without stopping)* It's Mrs. Buchanan. I've got to phone to the doctor. *(She hurries off.)*

Dick. *(as they approach the stoop)* Say, who's your little friend?

Mae. Oh, that's Rose Maurrant. She lives in the house.

Dick. She's kinda cute, ain't she?

Mae. *(seating herself on the stoop)* Say, accordin' to you, anythin' in a skirt is kinda cute — providin' the skirt is short enough.

Dick. Yeah, but they ain't any of 'em as cute as you, Mae.

Mae. *(yawning and scratching her leg)* Yeah?

Dick. Honest, I mean it. How 'bout a little kiss? *(He puts his arms about her and plants a long kiss upon her lips. She submits, with an air of intense boredom.)*

Dick. *(removing his lips)* Say, you might show a little en- thoo-siasm.

Mae. *(rouging her lips)* Say, you seem to think I oughta hang out a flag, every time some bozo decides to wipe off his mouth on me.

Dick. De trouble wit' you is you need another little snifter. *(He reaches for his flask.)*

Mae. Nope! I can't swaller any more o' that rotten gin o' yours.

Dick. Why, it ain't so worse. I don't mind it no more since I had that brass linin' put in me stomach. Well, happy days! *(He takes a long drink.)*

Mae. *(rising indignantly)* Hey, for God's sake, what are you doin' — emptyin' the flask?

Dick. *(removing the flask from his lips)* I t'ought you didn't want none.

MAE. Can't you take a joke? *(She snatches the flask from him and drains it, kicking out at DICK, to prevent his taking it from her.)*

DICK. *(snatching the empty flask)* Say, you wanna watch your step, baby, or you're li'ble to go right up in a puff o' smoke.

MAE. *(whistling)* Phew! Boy! I feel like a t'ree alarm fire! Say, what de hell do dey make dat stuff out of?

DICK. T'ree parts dynamite an' one part army mule. Dey use it for blastin' out West.

MAE. *(bursting raucously into a jazz tune)* Da-da-da-da-dee! Da-da-da-da-dee! *(She executes some dance steps.)*

DICK. Say, shut up, will ya? You'll be wakin' the whole neighborhood.

MAE. *(boisterously)* What the hell do I care? Da-da-da-da-dee! Da-da-da-da-dee! *(suddenly amorous, as she turns an unsteady pirouette)* Kiss me, kid!

DICK. I'll say! *(They lock in a long embrace.)*

(SAM, coatless, his shirt-collar open, appears at the window, watches the pair for a moment, and then turns away, obviously disgusted. They do not see him.)

DICK. *(taking MAE'S arm)* Come on!

MAE. Wait a minute! Where y' goin'?

DICK. Come on, I'm tellin' ya! Fred Hennessy gimme de key to his apartment. Dere won't be nobody dere.

MAE. *(protesting feebly)* I oughta go home. *(Her hand to her head.)* Oh, baby! Say, nail down dat sidewalk, will ya?

DICK. Come on!

(ROSE appears at the left.)

MAE. Sweet papa! *(She kisses DICK noisily; then bursts into song again.)* Da-da-da-da-dee! Da-da-da-da-dee! *(as they pass ROSE)* Hello, Rose, How's de milkman?

DICK. *(raising his hat with drunken politeness)* Goo' night, sweetheart. *(They go off, at the left, MAE'S snatches of song dying away in the distance. ROSE stands still, for a moment, choking back her mortification.)*

BUCHANAN'S VOICE. Miss Maurrant, did you get them?

ROSE. *(looking up)* Why yes, I did. The doctor will be here right away. And Mrs. Thomas said it would take her about an hour.

(VINCENT JONES appears at the right and stops near the stoop. He is a typical New York taxicab driver, in a cap. ROSE does not see him.)

BUCHANAN'S VOICE. She's got terrible pains. Your mother's up here, with her.

(MRS. BUCHANAN is heard calling faintly.)

BUCHANAN'S VOICE. I think she's calling me. *(ROSE goes towards the stoop and sees VINCENT.)*

VINCENT. Hello, Rosie.

ROSE. Good evening. *(She tries to pass, but he blocks her way.)*

VINCENT. What's your hurry?

ROSE. It's late.

VINCENT. You don' wanna go to bed, yet. Come on, I'll

take you for a ride in me hack. *(He puts his arm about her.)*

ROSE. Please let me pass.

(SAM appears at the window. They do not see him.)

VINCENT. *(enjoying ROSE'S struggle to escape)* You got a lot o' stren'th, ain't you? Say, do you know, you're gettin' fat? *(He passes one hand over her body.)*

ROSE. Let me go, you big tough.

SAM. *(simultaneously)* Take your hands off her! *(He climbs quickly out of the window and onto the stoop. VINCENT, surprised, releases ROSE and steps to the sidewalk. ROSE goes up the steps. SAM, trembling with excitement and fear, stands on the top step. VINCENT glowers up at him.)*

VINCENT. Well, look who's here! *(mockingly)* Haster gesehn de fish in de Bowery? *(menacingly)* What de hell do you want?

SAM. *(chokingly)* You keep your hands off her!

VINCENT. Yeah? *(sawing the air with his hands)* Oi, Jakie! *(He suddenly lunges forward, seizes SAM'S arm, pulls him violently by the right hand down the steps and swings him about, so that they stand face to face, to the left of the stoop. ROSE comes down between them.)* Now what o' ya got t' say?

ROSE. Let him alone!

SAM. *(inarticulately)* If you touch her again—

VINCENT. *(mockingly)* If I touch her again—! *(savagely)* Aw, shut up, you little kike bastard! *(He brushes ROSE aside and putting his open hand against SAM'S face, sends him sprawling to the pavement.)*

ROSE. *(Her fists clenched.)* You big coward.

VINCENT. *(standing over SAM)* Get up, why don't you?

ROSE. *(crossing to SAM)* If you hit him again, I'll call my father.

(MRS. JONES and the dog appear at the right.)

VINCENT. Gee, don't frighten me like dat. I got a weak heart. *(He is sobered, nevertheless. SAM picks himself up. As MRS. JONES approaches:)* Hello, ma.

MRS. JONES. *(with maternal pride)* Hello, Vincent. What's goin' on here?

VINCENT. Oh, jus' a little friendly argument. Ikey Finkelstein don't like me to say good evenin' to his girl friend.

ROSE. You'd better keep your hands to yourself, hereafter.

VINCENT. Is dat so? Who said so, huh?

MRS. JONES. Come on, Vincent. Come on upstairs. I saved some stew for you.

VINCENT. All right, I'm comin'. *(to ROSE:)* Good night, dearie. *(He makes a feint at SAM, who starts back in terror. VINCENT laughs.)*

MRS. JONES. Aw, let 'im alone, Vincent.

VINCENT. *(as he goes up the steps)* Who's touchin' him? A little cockroach like dat, ain't woit' my time. *(to ROSE:)* Some sheik you picked out for yourself! *(He Enters the vestibule and opens the door with his latchkey.)*

MRS. JONES. *(going up the steps)* You seem to have plenty of admirers, Miss Maurrant. *(pausing on the top step)* But I guess you come by it natural. *(ROSE does not reply. MRS. JONES follows VINCENT into the house. ROSE averts her head *to keep back the tears. SAM, stands facing the house, his whole body quivering with emotion. Suddenly he raises his arms, his fists clenched.)*

SAM. *(hysterically, as he rushes to the foot of the stoop)* The dirty bum! I'll kill him!

ROSE. *(turning and going to him)* It's all right, Sam. Never mind.

SAM. *(sobbing)* I'll kill him! I'll kill him! *(He throws himself on the stoop and, burying his head in his arms, sobs hysterically. ROSE sits beside him and puts her arm about him.)*

ROSE. It's all right, Sam. Everything's all right. Why should you pay any attention to a big tough like that? *(SAM does not answer. ROSE caresses his hair and he grows calmer.)* He's nothing but a loafer, you know that. What do you care what he says?

SAM. *(without raising his head)* I'm a coward.

ROSE. Why no, you're not, Sam.

SAM. Yes, I am. I'm a coward.

ROSE. Why, he's not worth your little finger, Sam. You wait and see. Ten years from now, he'll still be driving a taxi and you — why, you'll be so far above him, you won't even remember he's alive.

SAM. I'll never be anything.

ROSE. Why, don't talk like that, Sam. A boy with your brains and ability. Graduating from college with honors and all that! Why, if I were half as smart as you, I'd be just so proud of myself!

SAM. What's the good of having brains, if nobody ever looks at you — if nobody knows you exist?

ROSE. *(gently)* I know you exist, Sam.

SAM. It wouldn't take much to make you forget me.

Rose. I'm not so sure about that. Why do you say that, Sam?

Sam. Because I know. It's different with you. You have beauty — people look at you — you have a place in the world—

Rose. I don't know. It's not always so easy, being a girl — I often wish I were a man. It seems to me that when you're a man, it's so much easier to sort of — be yourself, to kind of be the way you feel. But when you're a girl, it's different. It doesn't seem to matter what you are, or what you're thinking or feeling — all that men seem to care about is just the one thing. And when you're sort of trying to find out, just where you're at, it makes it hard. Do you see what I mean? *(hesitantly)* Sam, there's something I want to ask you — *(She stops.)*

Sam. *(turning to her)* What is it, Rose?

Rose. I wouldn't dream of asking anybody but you. *(with a great effort)* Sam, do you think it's true — what they're saying about my mother? *(SAM averts his head, without answering.)*

Rose. *(wretchedly)* I guess it is, isn't it?

Sam. *(agitatedly)* They were talking here, before — I couldn't stand it any more! *(He clasps his head and, springing to his feet, goes to the right of the stoop.)* Oh, God, why do we go on living in this sewer?

Rose. *(appealingly)* What can I do, Sam? *(SAM makes a helpless gesture.)* You see, my father means well enough, and all that, but he's always been sort of strict and — I don't know — sort of making you freeze up, when you really wanted to be nice and loving. That's the whole trouble, I guess; my mother never had anybody to really love her. She's sort of gay and happy like — you know, she likes having a good time and all that. But my father is different. Only — the way things are now — everybody talking and making remarks, all the neighbors spying and whispering — it sort of makes me feel — *(She shudders.)* I don't know—!

SAM. *(coming over to her again)* I wish I could help you, Rose.

ROSE. You do help me, Sam — just by being nice and sympathetic and talking things over with me. There's so few people you can really talk to, do you know what I mean? Sometimes, I get the feeling that I'm all alone in the world and that—

(A scream of pain from MRS. BUCHANAN.)

ROSE. *(springing to her feet)* Oh, just listen to her!

SAM. Oh, God!

ROSE. The poor thing! She must be having terrible pains.

SAM. That's all there is in life — nothing but pain. From before we're born, until we die! Everywhere you look, oppression and cruelty! If it doesn't come from nature, it comes from humanity — humanity trampling on itself and tearing at its own throat. The whole world is nothing but a blood stained arena, filled with misery and suffering. It's too high a price to pay for life — life isn't worth it! *(He seats himself despairingly on the stoop.)*

ROSE. *(putting her hand on his shoulder)* Oh, I don't know, Sam. I feel blue and discouraged, sometimes, too. And I get a sort of feeling of, oh, what's the use. Like last night. I hardly slept all night, on account of the heat and on account of thinking about — well, all sorts of things. And this morning, when I got up, I felt so miserable. Well, all of a sudden, I decided I'd walk to the office. And when I got to the Park, everything looked so green and fresh, that I got a kind of feeling of, well, maybe it's not so bad, after all. And then, what do you think? — all of a sudden, I saw a big lilac bush, with some flowers still on it. It made me think about the poem you said for me — remember? — the one about the lilacs.

SAM. *(quoting)*

"When lilacs last in the dooryard bloom'd

And the great star early droop'd in the western sky in the night,

I mourn'd and yet shall mourn, with ever-returning Spring."

(He repeats the last line.)

I mourn'd and yet shall mourn, with ever-returning Spring? Yes!

ROSE. No, not that part. I mean the part about the farmhouse. Say it for me, Sam. *(She sits at his feet.)*

SAM.

"In the door-yard, fronting an old farmhouse, near the white-washed palings,

Stands the lilac bush, tall growing, with heart shaped leaves of rich green,

With many a pointed blossom, rising delicate, with the perfume strong I love,

With every leaf a miracle — and from this bush in the door yard,

With delicate color'd blossoms and heart shaped leaves of rich green,

A sprig with its flower I break."

Rose. *(eagerly)* Yes, that's it! That's just what I felt like doing — breaking off a little bunch of the flowers. But then I thought, maybe a policeman or somebody would see me, and then I'd get into trouble; so I didn't.

Buchanan's Voice. Miss Maurrant! Miss Maurrant! *(SAM and ROSE spring to their feet and look up.)*

Rose. Yes?

Buchanan's Voice. Do you mind phoning to the doctor again? She's getting worse.

Rose. Yes, sure I will. *(She starts to go.)* Wait! Maybe this is the doctor now.

(DR. WILSON appears at the left.)

Buchanan's Voice. *(excitedly as DR. WILSON appears at the left)* Yes, that's him. Mrs. Maurrant! Tell her the doctor's here! Doctor, I guess you're none too soon.

Dr. Wilson. *(a seedy, middle aged man in a crumpled Panama)* Plenty of time. Just don't get excited. *(He throws away his cigarette and Enters the vestibule. The mechanical clicking of the door latch is heard as DR. WILSON goes into the house.)*

Rose. I hope she won't have to suffer much longer.

(MAURRANT appears at the window, in his under shirt.)

Maurrant. Rose!

Rose. *(rather startled)* Yes, pop, I'll be right up.

Maurrant. Well, don't be makin' me call you again, d'ya hear?

Rose. I'm coming right away. *(MAURRANT leaves the window.)*

Rose. I'd better go up now, Sam.

Sam. Do you have to go to bed, when you're told, like a child?

Rose. I know, Sam, but there's so much wrangling goes on, all the time, as it is, what's the use of having any more? Good night, Sam. There was something I wanted to talk to you about, but it will have to be another time. *(She holds out her hand. SAM takes it and holds it in his.)*

Sam. *(trembling and rising to his feet)* Rose, will you kiss me?

Rose. *(simply)* Why, of course I will, Sam. *(She offers him her lips. He clasps her in a fervent embrace, to which she submits but does not respond.)*

Rose. *(freeing herself gently)* Don't be discouraged about things, Sam. You wait and see — you're going to do big things, some day. I've got lots of confidence in you.

Sam. *(turning away his head)* I wonder if you really have, Rose?

Rose. Why, of course, I have! And don't forget it! Good night. I hope it won't be too hot to sleep.

Sam. Good night, Rose. *(He watches her, as she opens the door with her latch key and goes into the house. Then he goes to the stoop and seating himself, falls into a reverie.)*

(A POLICEMAN appears at the right and strolls across, but SAM is oblivious to him. In the distance, a home comer sings drunkenly. A light appears, in the Maurrant hall bedroom, and a moment later, ROSE comes to the window and leans out.)

Rose. *(calling softly)* Hoo-hoo! Sam! *(SAM looks up, then rises.)* Good night, Sam. *(She wafts him a kiss.)*

SAM. *(with deep feeling)* Good night, Rose dear. *(She smiles at him. then she pulls down the shade. SAM looks up for a moment, then resumes his seat.)*

(A scream from MRS. BUCHANAN makes him shudder. A deep rhythmic snoring emanates from the Fiorentino apartment. A steamboat whistle is heard. The snoring in the Fiorentino apartment continues. SAM raises his clenched hands to heaven. A distant clock begins to strike twelve. SAM'S arms and head drop forward.)

(THE CURTAIN FALLS SLOWLY.)

ACT TWO

Daybreak, the next morning. It is still quite dark and comparatively quiet. The rhythmic snoring in the Fiorentino apartment is still heard, and now and then, a distant "L" train or speeding automobile. A moment after the rise of the curtain, JONES appears, at the right, on his way home from the speakeasy. He reels, slightly, but negotiates the steps and entrance door, without too much difficulty. It grows lighter — and noisier. The street light goes out. The Olsen baby begins to cry. An alarm clock rings. A dog barks. A canary begins to sing. Voices are heard in the distance. They die out and other voices are heard. The house door opens and DR. WILSON comes out, passing JONES, at the top of the stoop. DR. WILSON stands on the steps and yawns the yawn of an over tired man. Then he lights a cigarette and goes towards the left.

BUCHANAN'S VOICE. Doctor!

DR. WILSON. *(stopping and looking up)* Well?

BUCHANAN'S VOICE. What if she does wake up?

DR. WILSON. *(sharply)* She won't, I've told you! She's too exhausted. The best thing you can do is lie down and get some sleep yourself.

(As he goes off at the left, MAE and DICK appear. They walk slowly and listlessly and far apart.)

66

DICK. *(as they reach the stoop)* Well, goo' night.

MAE. *(with a yawn, as she finds her latch key)* Goo' night. *(going up the steps and looking towards the Fiorentino apartment)* Aw, shut up, you wop!

DICK. *(his dignity wounded)* How 'bout kissin' me goodnight?

MAE. *(venomously, from the top step)* For God's sake, ain't you had enough kissin' for one night! *(She Enters the vestibule and puts the key in the lock.)*

(The ringing of an alarm clock is heard.)

DICK. *(raising his voice)* Well, say, if that's the way you feel about it—

MAE. Aw, go to hell! *(She Enters the house. The alarm clock has stopped ringing.)*

DICK. You dirty little tart!

(He stands, muttering to himself, for a moment, then goes off at the right, passing the POLICEMAN, who looks at him, suspiciously. The sounds of a Swedish quarrel are heard from the janitor's apartment. The baby is still crying. As the POLICEMAN goes left, a MILKMAN appears, whistling and carrying a rack of full milk bottles.)

THE POLICEMAN. Hello, Louie. *(The snoring in the Fiorentino apartment stops.)*

THE MILKMAN. Hello, Harry. Goin' to be another scorcher.

THE POLICEMAN. You said it. *(He goes off at the left.)*

(The MILKMAN crosses to the cellar steps. MAE appears, at the hall bedroom window of the Jones apartment, and removes her dress over her head. The MILKMAN, about to go down the steps, sees her and stops to watch. MAE, about to slip out of her step-in, sees him, throws him an angry look and pulls down the shade. The MILKMAN grins and goes down the cellar steps. CHARLIE HILDEBRAND comes out of the house. He is chewing gum and as he comes out to the top of the stoop, he scatters the wrappings of the stick of gum on the stoop. Then he jumps down the four steps of the stoop, in one jump, and goes off at the left, pulling the chewing gum out in a long ribbon and carefully avoiding all the cracks in the pavement. A YOUNG WORKMAN, carrying a kit of tools and a tin lunchbox, appears at the left, extinguishes the red light on the excavation, and opening the door, goes in. A TRAMP comes on at the right and shuffles across. He sees a cigar butt on the pavement, picks it up and pockets it, as he exits at the left. ROSE, in her nightgown, appears at the window, yawns slightly and disappears. It is daylight now. The baby stops crying. MRS. OLSEN comes up the cellar steps. She goes up the stoop, turns out the light in the vestibule, and takes the door off the latch. The MILKMAN comes up the cellar steps, his tray laden with empty bottles and goes off, whistling, at the left. SAM, coatless, a book in his hand, appears at the window. He looks out for a moment, then climbs out on the stoop, looks up at ROSE'S window, then seats himself and begins to read. WILLIE comes out of the house.)

WILLIE. *(chanting, as he comes down the steps)* Fat, Fat the water rat, Fifty bullets in his hat.

SAM. Hello, Willie. Is Rose up yet?

WILLIE. *(without stopping or looking at him)* Yeah. I don't know. I guess so. *(He turns a somersault and goes off at left, continuing his chanting. SAM glances up at ROSE'S window again, then resumes his book.)*

(MRS. JONES and her dog come out of the house.)

MRS. JONES. *(haughtily, as she comes down the steps)* Mornin'.

SAM. *(scarcely looking up from his book)* Good morning. *(MRS. JONES and the dog go off at the right.)*

(A middle aged WORKMAN, carrying a large coil of wire, appears at the left and goes to the door of the excavation. MRS. OLSEN comes out of the house and Exits into the basement.)

THE WORKMAN. *(calling)* You down there, Eddie?

A VOICE. *(from the depths)* Yeah!

THE WORKMAN. All right! *(He climbs down into the excavation.)*

(ROSE comes to window and pulls up the shade. WILLIE and CHARLIE can be heard, offstage left, engaged in an earnest conversation.)

CHARLIE. *(offstage)* He could not!

WILLIE. *(offstage)* He could so! *(They appear at left. Each has under his arm, a paperbag, from which a loaf of bread protrudes.)*

CHARLIE. I'll betcha he couldn't.

WILLIE. I'll betcha he could.

CHARLIE. I'll betcha a million dollars he couldn't.

WILLIE. I'll betcha five million dollars he could. Hold

that! *(He hands CHARLIE his loaf of bread and turns a cart-wheel.)* Bet you can't do it.

CHARLIE. Bet I can. *(He puts both loaves of bread on the pavement, attempts a cart-wheel and fails.)*

WILLIE. *(laughing raucously)* Haw-haw! Told you you couldn't!

CHARLIE. Can you do this? *(He turns a back somersault.)*

WILLIE. Sure — easy! *(He turns a back somersault. They pick up their loaves again. WILLIE'S drops out of the bag, but he dusts it, with his hand, and replaces it.)* How many steps can you jump up?

CHARLIE. Three. *(He jumps up three steps.)*

WILLIE. I can do four.

CHARLIE. Let's see you. *(WILLIE, the bread under his arm, jumps up the four steps, undisturbed by SAM'S presence. He drops the bread, and is about to replace it in the bag, but gets a better idea. He inflates the bag and explodes it with a blow of his fist. CHARLIE looks on, in admiration and envy.)*

(ROSE appears at the window.)

ROSE. Willie, we're waiting for the bread.

WILLIE. *(holding it up)* All right! Cantcha see I got it? *(He Enters the house, followed by CHARLIE.)*

SAM. *(rising)* Hello, Rose.

ROSE. Hello, Sam.

SAM. Come down.

ROSE. I haven't had breakfast yet. *(calling into the room)* Yes! He's on his way up.

(MISS CUSHING comes out of the house.)

MISS CUSHING. Good morning. *(She looks inquiringly from SAM to ROSE.)*

SAM. *(impatiently)* Good morning.

(A middle aged man appears at the right, accompanied by a scrawny child of about fourteen. They walk across the stage.)

ROSE. Good morning, Miss Cushing. *(MISS CUSHING goes off, at the left, glancing back at ROSE and SAM.)*

ROSE. I'm going to Mr. Jacobson's funeral. *(calling into the room)* Yes, I'm coming. *(to SAM:)* Breakfast's ready. I'll be down as soon as the dishes are done.

(She disappears. SAM looks up at the window, for a moment, then begins to read again. MRS. FIORENTINO appears at the window, at the extreme left, with a double armful of bedding, which she deposits upon the window sill. Then she goes away again. SHIRLEY appears at the window.)

SHIRLEY. Sam, breakfast is ready.

SAM. I don't want any breakfast.

SHIRLEY. What do you mean, you don't want any breakfast? What kind of a business is that, not to eat breakfast?

SAM. Do I have to eat breakfast, if I don't want to?

SHIRLEY. You've got your head so full of that Rose Maurrant upstairs, that you don't want to eat or sleep or anything, any more.

SAM. If I don't feel like eating, why should I eat? *(burst-*

ing out) You're always telling me: "Eat!" "Don't eat!" "Get up!" "Go to bed!" I know what I want to do, without being told.

SHIRLEY. I don't see, just when you're graduating from college, why you want to get mixed up with a little bat-zimer like that!

SAM. It's always the same thing over again with you. You never can get over your race prejudice. I've told you a hundred times that the Jews are no better than anybody else.

SHIRLEY. I'm not talking about that! Look at the kind of family she comes from. What's her father? Nothing but an illiterate rough neck. And her mother—

SAM. *(indignantly)* Are you starting, too?

KAPLAN'S VOICE. Shoi-ley!

SHIRLEY. Wait a minute, papa's calling. *(into the room)* All right, papa! *(to SAM:)* Come in, Sam, or papa will be making long speeches again.

SAM. *(impatiently)* All right! All right! I'll come.

(A young shopgirl, smiling to herself, appears at the right and walks across the stage. SAM rises and goes into the house. SHIRLEY leaves the window. BUCHANAN, emerging from the house, collarless and unshaven, encounters SAM in the vestibule.)

BUCHANAN. *(eagerly)* Good morning!

SAM. *(abruptly)* Good morning. *(He Enters the house. BUCHANAN looks back at him, then comes down the steps.*

(MRS. FIORENTINO raises the drawn shade and opens the window.)

MRS. FIORENTINO. Good morning, Mr. Buchanan.

BUCHANAN. Oh, good morning, Mrs. Fiorentino. *(going over to the left balustrade)* I guess you know that the baby came last night, don't you?

MRS. FIORENTINO. No! I did not hear a vord about it.

BUCHANAN. Why, I thought she'd wake up the whole neighborhood, the way she was yelling. Three-thirty this morning, the baby came. I been up the whole night.

(An old LETTER-CARRIER, coatless, appears at the right.)

MRS. FIORENTINO. A boy, is it?

BUCHANAN. No, it's a little girl. I guess we'll call her Mary, after my mother.

LETTER-CARRIER. *(going up the steps)* Mornin'.

MRS. FIORENTINO. Good morning. Any letters for me?

LETTER-CARRIER. *(from the top of the steps)* No, not a thing.

BUCHANAN. *(turning toward him)* I was just telling Mrs. Fiorentino, I had a little addition to my family last night.

LETTER-CARRIER. Your first, is it?

BUCHANAN. *(hastening to explain)* Well, we've only been married a little over a year.

LETTER-CARRIER. Well, I've had seven, an' I'm still luggin' a mail bag at sixty-two. *(He goes into the vestibule and puts the mail into the letter boxes.)*

MRS. FIORENTINO. How is your wife?

BUCHANAN. Well, she had a pretty hard time of it. Her

sister's up there with her. And Mrs. Maurrant was up, nearly all night. I don't know what we'd have done without her.

LETTER-CARRIER. *(coming down the steps)* It don't pay to let 'em have their own way, too much. That's where I made my mistake.

(As the LETTER-CARRIER goes off, at the left, LIPPO appears at the window behind his wife, and tickles her.)

MRS. FIORENTINO. *(startled)* Lippo!

BUCHANAN. Morning. I was just telling your wife—

MRS. FIORENTINO. Lippo, what do you think? Mr. Buchanan has a little girl!

LIPPO. Ah, dosta fine! Margherita, why you don't have da baby, ha?

MRS. FIORENTINO. *(abruptly)* I must go and make the coffee. *(She goes away from the window.)*

(OLSEN comes half way up the steps and leans against the railing, smoking his pipe.)

A VOICE. *(offstage left)* Oh-h! Corn! Sweet corn!

LIPPO. Ees funny t'ing. You gotta da leetle, skeeny wife an she's hava da baby. My Margherita, she's beeg an' fat an' she no can hava da baby.

BUCHANAN. Well, that's the way o' the world, I guess.

(As he goes off, at the left, an ICE-MAN appears, trundling a three-wheeled cart, filled with ice.)

LIPPO. Buon giorno, Mike.

MIKE. Buon giorno, signore. Come sta?

LIPPO. Benissimo. Fa molto caldo ancora, oggi.

MIKE. Si, si, signore. Bisognera abbastanza ghiaccio. Twen'y fi' cent, ha?

LIPPO. No, no, e troppo.

MIKE. Twen'y cent? Eesa melta fas'.

LIPPO. Alla right. Gimme twen'y cent.

MIKE. Si, si, signore. Sure.

(As he wheels the cart to the cellar entrance and begins to chop a block of ice, a MAN in shirt sleeves strides in from the left and stops at the curb, as though seeing someone in a house across the street.)

THE MAN. *(angrily)* Well, what about it? We've been waiting a half an hour!

A VOICE. I'll be right over!

THE MAN. Yeah? Well, make it snappy! *(He strides off at the left, muttering angrily.)*

(ROSE comes out of the house and stands in the doorway, looking for SAM. Then she comes out on the stoop and peers into the Kaplan apartment. As she turns away, she sees LIPPO.)

ROSE. *(crossing to the left of the stoop)* Good morning.

LIPPO. Gooda mornin', Meesa Maurrant. *(MIKE goes down the cellar with a chunck of ice.)*

ROSE. It's awful hot again, isn't it?

LIPPO. You don' like?

ROSE. I don't sleep very well, when it's so hot.

LIPPO. No? Ahm sleepa fine. Een Eetaly, where Ahm born, is much more 'ot like 'ere. Een summer, ess too 'ot for workin'. Ees too 'ot only for sleepin'. W'en Ahm leetla boy, Ahm sleepa, sleepa, whola day. I don't wear no clo's—nawthin' only leetle short pair pants. I lay down on groun' under da lemon-tree, Ahm sleepa whola day.

ROSE. Under a lemon-tree! That must have been nice.

LIPPO. Ees smella sweet, lemon-tree. Where Ahm born ees t'ousan' lemon-tree. Lemon an' olive an' arancia.

ROSE. Oh, that must be lovely!

LIPPO. Ah, ees bew-tiful! Ees most bewtiful place in whole worl'. You hear about Sorrent', ha?

ROSE. No, I don't think I ever did.

LIPPO. (incredulously) You never hear about Sorrent'?

ROSE. No, I don't know much about geography. Is it a big place?

LIPPO. Ees not vera beeg—but ever'body know Sorrent'. Sorrento gentile! La bella Sorrento! You hear about Napoli—Baia di Napoli?

ROSE. Oh yes, the Bay of Naples! Is it near there?

LIPPO. Sure, ees on Bay of Napoli. Ees bew-tiful! Ees alla blue. Sky blue, water blue, sun ees shine alla time.

ROSE. Oh, how lovely.

(MIKE comes up the cellar-steps, chops another block of ice, and goes down the cellar-steps with it.)

Lippo. An' ees Vesuvio, too. You hear about Vesuvio?—ees beeg volcano.

Rose. Oh yes, sure. I saw a picture once, called The Last Days of Pompeii, and it showed Mount Vesuvius, with smoke coming out of the top.

Lippo. Da's right. An' night-time, ees fire come out, maka da sky red.

Rose. Didn't it frighten you?

Lippo. Ah no, ees nawthin' to be afraid. Ees jus' volcano.

Rose. I'd love to go to Italy. It must be awfully pretty. But I don't suppose I ever will.

Lippo. W'y sure! Some day you gonna marry reech fella; 'e's taka you Eetaly—ever'where.

Rose. I guess there's not much chance of that. Rich fellows aren't going around looking for girls like me to marry. Anyhow, I don't think money is everything, do you?

Lippo. Ees good to hava money. Da's w'y Ahm come to America. Een Eetaly, ees bewtiful, but ees no money. 'Ere ees not bewtiful, but ees plenty money. Ees better to 'ave money.

(An elderly MAN, in the gray uniform of a special officer, comes out of the house, filling his pipe from a tobacco-box.)

The Man. Good mornin'.

Rose. Good morning, Mr. Callahan. *(The MAN drops the empty tobacco-tin on the sidewalk and goes off slowly at the left.)* I don't think I'd be happy, just marrying a man with money, if I didn't care for him, too.

LIPPO. *(laughing)* Wotsa matter, ha? You lova da leetla kike, ha?

ROSE. Why no, I don't. I don't love anybody—at least, I don't think I do. But it's not on account of his being a Jew.

LIPPO. No, ees no good—Jew. 'E's only t'ink about money, money—alla time money.

ROSE. But Sam isn't like that, a bit. He's only interested in poetry and things like that.

(The ICE-MAN comes up out of the cellar and trundles off his cart at the right.)

MRS. FIORENTINO. *(calling)* Lippo! Breakfast!

LIPPO. *(calling)* Alla right, Margherita! *(To ROSE:)* You marry fella wit' lot o' money. Ees much better. *(He goes away from the window.)*

(MISS CUSHING appears, at the left, carrying a paper-bag.)

ROSE. How's your mother today, Miss Cushing?

MISS CUSHING. She's not feeling so good today.

ROSE. It's too bad she's not feeling well.

MISS CUSHING. I'm afraid it's her heart. At her age, you know—! *(She Enters the house.)*

(Two COLLEGE GIRLS of nineteen appear at the right.)

FIRST GIRL. *(as they appear)* I don't understand it.

SECOND GIRL. Convex is this way; concave is this way.

FIRST GIRL. That I know.

SECOND GIRL. When you're near-sighted, they give you convex glasses, and when you're far-sighted, they give you concave.

FIRST GIRL. That I didn't know.

SECOND GIRL. Of course, you know it. Didn't we have it in psychology?

FIRST GIRL. *(as they disappear at the left)* I don't remember.

(WILLY comes out of the house, on his way to school. He is hatless, and carries his books under his arm.)

ROSE. *(intercepting him at the top of the stoop)* Why, Willie, the way you look! Your collar's all open.

WILLIE. I know it! De button came off.

ROSE. Why didn't you ask ma to sew it on for you?

WILLIE. She ain't dere. She's up at Buchanan's.

ROSE. Well, wait till I see if I have a pin. *(She searches in her hand-bag.)*

WILLIE. *(starting down the steps)* Aw, it's all right de way it is.

ROSE. *(following him to the sidewalk)* No, it isn't. You can't go to school like that. *(producing a safety-pin)* Now, hold still, while I fix it.

WILLIE. *(squirming)* Aw, fer de love o' Mike—!

ROSE. You'll get stuck, if you don't hold still. There, that looks better, now. And you didn't comb your hair, either.

WILLIE. *(trying to escape)* Say, lemme alone, cantcha?

ROSE. *(taking a comb out of her hand-bag and combing his*

hair) You can't go to school looking like a little street-loafer.

WILLIE. Aw, you gimmie a pain in de—

ROSE. You're getting big enough to comb your own hair, without being told. There! Now you look very nice.

WILLIE. So's your old man! *(He runs towards the left kicking the empty tobacco tin ahead of him, then stops, turns and deliberately rumples his hair.)*

ROSE. *(indignantly, as WILLIE runs off)* Why, Willie!

(MRS. JONES and the dog appear at the right. OLSEN knocks the ashes out of his pipe and goes down into the cellar. MRS. MAURRANT comes out of the house.)

ROSE. Hello, ma.

MRS. JONES. *(at the steps)* Good mornin'.

ROSE and MRS. MAURRANT. Good morning, Mrs. Jones.

MRS. JONES. How's little Mrs. Buchanan gettin' on?

MRS. MAURRANT. Well, she's sleeping now, poor thing. She was so worn out, she just went off into a sound sleep. I really didn't think last night, she'd have the strength to pull through it.

MRS. JONES. Well, it's somethin', we all got to go through. I been through enough with mine, I hope to tell you. Not that they didn't turn out all right.

MRS. MAURRANT. I wouldn't give up having mine for anything in the world.

MRS. JONES. Well, after all, what more does any woman want than watchin' her kids grow up an' a husband to look out for her?

MRS. MAURRANT. Yes, that's true.

MRS. JONES. Yes, and the world would be a whole lot better off, if there was more that lived up to it. *(starting up the steps)* Well, I gotta get my Mae up out o' bed. Gawd knows what time she got in, this mornin'. *(She Enters the vestibule, then stops and turns.)* If you don't mind my bein' so bold, Mrs. Maurrant — an' I don't mind sayin' it in front of your daughter, either — I'd think twice before I'd let any child o' mine bring a Jew into the family.

ROSE. *(with a show of temper)* I don't see what it has to do with you, Mrs. Jones.

MRS. JONES. There's no need to get huffy about it. I'm only advisin' you for your own good. I'm sure it don't make no difference to me what you do. Come on, Queenie. *(She goes into the house.)*

ROSE. Well, of all the nerve I ever heard in my life—! She and those wonderful children of hers!

MRS. MAURRANT. *(coming half way down the steps)* The best way is not to pay any attention to her. There's lots of people like that, in the world — they never seem to be happy, unless they're making trouble for somebody. Did Willie go to school?

ROSE. Yes, he did. It's awful the way he goes around, looking like a little tough. And the language he uses, too.

MRS. MAURRANT. I know. I just don't seem able to manage him, any more.

ROSE. I sometimes wonder if it wouldn't be better for us all, if we moved out to the suburbs somewhere — you know, some place in Jersey or Staten Island.

Mrs. Maurrant. I don't think pop would do it.

(MAURRANT comes out of the house, carrying a much battered satchel.)

Mrs. Maurrant. Are you leaving now, Frank?

Maurrant. *(from the top of the stoop)* Looks like it, don't it. Where you been all this while?

Mrs. Maurrant. Why, you know where I've been, Frank — up to Mrs. Buchanan's.

Maurrant. Yeah? An' where you goin' now?

Mrs. Maurrant. Just around to Kraus's to get a chicken. I thought I'd make her some chicken soup, to give her strength.

Maurrant. Say, how about lookin' after your own home an' lettin' the Buchanans look after theirs.

Mrs. Maurrant. All I'm trying to do is to be a little neighborly. It's the least anybody can do, with the poor thing hardly able to lift her hand.

Maurrant. That's all right about that! *(coming down the steps)* A woman's got a right to stay in her own home, lookin' after her husband an' children.

Mrs. Maurrant. *(going towards him)* What else have I been doing all these years, I'd like to know?

Maurrant. Well, just see that you don't forget it, that's all — or there's li'ble to be trouble.

Mrs. Maurrant. *(putting her hand on his arm)* All right, Frank. Don't say any more, please. When will you be back — to-morrow?

Maurrant. I don' know when I'll be back. Whenever I'm t'roo wit' me work — that's when. What are you so anxious to know for, huh?

MRS. MAURRANT. Why, I just asked, that's all.

MAURRANT. Oh, you just asked, huh? Just in case somebody wanted to come aroun' callin', is that it?

MRS. MAURRANT. No, it isn't. It isn't anything of the kind. You got no right to talk to me like that, in front of my own daughter. You got no right. No, you haven't! *(She turns away and hurries off, abruptly, at the left.)*

ROSE. Ma! *(She starts to run after her mother.)*

MAURRANT. *(imperiously)* Come back here, you! *(ROSE hesitates.)* Come back, hear me? *(ROSE turns and comes slowly back.)* You stay right here. *(He puts down his satchel and takes a flask from his pocket.)*

ROSE. Why do you talk to her like that?

MAURRANT. Nobody's askin' you.

ROSE. If you were only a little nicer to her, maybe everything would be different.

MAURRANT. Yeah? Where's she got any kick comin'. Ain't I always been a good husband to her? Ain't I always looked after her? *(He takes a drink.)*

ROSE. It's not that, pop. It's somebody to be sort of nice to her that she wants — sort of nice and gentle, the way she is to you. That's all it is.

MAURRANT. *(turning to her)* So she's got you headed the same way, has she? Goin' out nights with married men, huh?

ROSE. You don't need to worry about me, pop. I can take care of myself, all right.

MAURRANT. No daughter o' mine ain't gonna go that way. I seen too many o' those kind around the theayter.

ROSE. Things are different, nowadays, Pop. I guess maybe you don't realize that. Girls aren't the way they used to be — sort of soft and helpless. A girl nowadays knows how to look out for herself. But not her, pop; she needs somebody to look after her.

MAURRANT. Aw, can all that talk! You been listenin' to them bolshevikis, that's the trouble. But I'm gonna keep you straight, by God, or I'll know the reason why.

ROSE. I guess I've got a right to think about things for myself.

MAURRANT. Yeah? Well, don't let me ketch that other bozo comin' around here, either — that's all I got to say.

ROSE. (hesitantly, going up to him) Pop, listen — couldn't we get a little house somewhere — Queens or somewhere like that?

MAURRANT. What's the idea?

ROSE. Well, I don't know. I sort of thought it would be nice for all of us. And maybe if ma had a nice little home and some real nice neighbors — do you see what I mean?

MAURRANT. This place suits me all right.

ROSE. You can get some real nice little houses, that don't cost such an awful lot. and I wouldn't mind helping to pay for it. And once we had it all fixed up—

MAURRANT. Forget it! I don' know when I'll be back. (as he starts to go right) An' remember what I tol' you, hear?

(MRS. JONES appears at her window, with a tin dust pan.)

MRS. JONES. Good mornin', Mr. Maurrant. You off on a little trip?

MAURRANT. *(curtly)* Yeah. *(He goes off. MRS. JONES empties the dust pan out of the window and goes away.)*

(KAPLAN comes out of the house, a bundle of newspapers, under his arm. He walks slowly and painfully, with the aid of a heavy stick.)

KAPLAN. *(at the foot of the steps)* Vy do you look so sed, hm?

ROSE. *(turning, and sitting on the right balustrade)* Oh, good morning, Mr. Kaplan.

KAPLAN. A young girl, like you, should not look so sed.

ROSE. I'm not sad, especially, only—

KAPLAN. You got troubles, hm?

ROSE. I don't know. It's just sort of everything.

KAPLAN. Velt-schmerz you got, hm? Vit' my boy Sem is de same t'ing. Dees vay you feel only ven you are yong. Ven you gat old like me, you tink only: "Much longer I von't be ehre."

ROSE. Why should things be the way they are, Mr. Kaplan? Why must people always be fighting and having troubles, instead of just sort of being happy together.

KAPLAN. My dear yong leddy, ef I could enser dis quastion, I would be de greatest benefactor thet de verld hes ever known. dees is som't'ing, vich all de philosophers hev been unable to enser. De ones thet believe in God, say de davil is responsible; and de ones they don't believe in God, say 'uman nature is responsible. It is my opinion

thet most unheppiness can be traced to economic cosses
and thet—

*(CHARLIE and MARY HILDEBRAND have come out of the
house, carrying their school books.)*

MARY. Hello.

ROSE. Hello, Mary. Hello, Charlie.

CHARLIE. Hello.

MARY. *(chattily, as they reach the sidewalk)* We're going to
be dispossessed today.

ROSE. What a shame!

MARY. Yes, ma'am. My father went away and so we
couldn't pay the rent.

CHARLIE. *(tugging at her arm)* Aw, come on, Mary.

ROSE. Have you another place to live, Mary?

MARY. No ma'am. But Miss Simpson, from the
Charities, says she'll find us a place. She says we must
learn to be less extavagant.

CHARLIE. Come ahead, will you?

MARY. I'm going to school now. Good-bye.

ROSE. Good-bye. *(The children go off, at the left.)*

KAPLAN. More troubles!

ROSE. I know. Isn't it awful to think of them being
turned out in the street like that?

KAPLAN. In a ciwilized verld, soch t'ings could not
heppen.

ROSE. You mean if there were different laws?

KAPLAN. Not laws! We got already too many laws. Ve
must hev ection, not laws. De verking klesses must t'row
off de yoke of ke*pit*alism, and ebolish wage slavery.

Rose. But wouldn't people still be unkind to each other and fight and quarrel among themselves?

Kaplan. My dear young leddy, so long as ve keep men in slevery, dey vill behave like sleves. But wance ve establish a verld based upon 'uman needs and not upon 'uman greed—

Rose. You mean people will begin being nice to each other and making allowances and all?

Kaplan. All dees vill come. Wot ve hev now is a wicious soicle. On de one hend, ve hev a rotten economic system—

Rose. Excuse me, here's my mother.

(She goes towards the left, as MRS. MAURRANT approaches, a paper package in her hand. KAPLAN goes off, at the right.)

Mrs. Maurrant. *(as ROSE comes up to her)* Did he go? *(They stop on the pavement, at the left of the stoop.)*

Rose. Yes.

Mrs. Maurrant. I got a little chicken, to make Mrs. Buchanan some soup.

Rose. He had a flask with him, ma. I hope he doesn't start drinking.

Mrs. Maurrant. What did he say — anything?

Rose. No, only the way he always talks. I tried to talk to him about buying a house, somewheres, but he wouldn't listen.

Mrs. Maurrant. No, I knew he wouldn't.

Rose. It doesn't seem to be any use trying to get him to listen to anything.

Mrs. Maurrant. It's always been that way. I've always

tried to be a good wife to him, Rose, But it never seemed to make any difference to him.

Rose. I know, ma.

Mrs. Maurrant. And I've tried to be a good mother, too.

Rose. I know, ma. I know just the way you feel about it.

Mrs. Maurrant. *(appealingly)* Do you, Rose?

Rose. Yes, ma, I do. Honest I do.

Mrs. Maurrant. I've always tried to make a nice home for him and to do what's right. But it doesn't seem to be any use.

Rose. I know, ma. *(hesitantly)* But it's on account of — *(She stops.)*

Mrs. Maurrant. Are you going to start, too? Are you going to start like all the others? *(She turns away and bursts into tears.)*

Rose. *(fondling her)* Don't ma. Please don't.

Mrs. Maurrant. I thought you'd be the one that would feel different.

Rose. I do, ma — really I do.

Mrs. Maurrant. What's the good of being alive, if you can't get a little something out of life? You might just as well be dead.

Rose. Look out, ma. Somebody's coming.

(A smartly dressed girl, with one side of her face covered with cotton and adhesive tape, appears at the left and crosses the stage. At the same time, JONES comes out of the house. ROSE and MRS. MAURRANT stand in awkward silence, as he comes down the stoop and approaches them.)

JONES. Well, is it hot enough for you, today?

ROSE. It's awful, isn't it?

JONES. *(as he goes towards the left)* You said it. Still along about January, we'll all be wishin' we had a little o' this weather. *(He Exits. MRS. MAURRANT goes towards the stoop.)*

ROSE. Ma, listen. If I say something, will you listen to me?

MRS. MAURRANT. Yes, sure I will, Rose. I'll listen to anything you say, only—

ROSE. Well, what I was thinking was, if he didn't come around here so much, maybe. Do you see what I mean, ma?

MRS. MAURRANT. *(constrainedly)* Yes, Rose.

ROSE. *(putting her arm around her)* It's on account of all that's going around — everybody in the whole house. You see what I mean, don't you, ma?

MRS. MAURRANT. Every person in the world has to have somebody to talk to. You can't live without somebody to talk to. I'm not saying that I can't talk to you, Rose, but you're only a young girl and it's not the same thing.

ROSE. It's only on account of pop. I'm scared of what he's likely to do, if he starts drinking.

MRS. MAURRANT. Well, I'll see, Rose. Sometimes I think I'd be better off if I was dead.

ROSE. If there was only something I could do.

MRS. MAURRANT. There isn't anything anybody could do. It's just the way things are, that's all.

(BUCHANAN appears at the left. They turn and face him, as he approaches.)

MRS. MAURRANT. Oh, Mr. Buchanan, I got a little chicken, so that I could make her some good, nourishing soup.

BUCHANAN. Well, say, you got to let me pay you for it.

MRS. MAURRANT. Oh, never mind about that. We'll have the chicken for supper tonight. Did you have her medicine made up?

BUCHANAN. Yes, I got it right here. I called up the office and they told me not to come down today.

MRS. MAURRANT. Well, that's very nice. It'll be a comfort to her to have you around.

BUCHANAN. Yes, that's what I thought, too. Well, I'd better be getting upstairs. *(He goes up the steps.)*

MRS. MAURRANT. I'll be up later, with the soup.

BUCHANAN. Well, thanks. *(stopping at the top of the stoop and turning to her)* You've been a mighty good neighbor, Mrs. Maurrant. *(He Enters the house.)*

MRS. MAURRANT. He's an awful nice, young feller — so nice and gentle. And he's always trying to be so helpful. It makes you feel sort of sorry for him.

(SHIRLEY comes out of the house, carrying a large wicker bag, which contains her lunch and school books. She takes a post card out of the mailbox.)

MRS. MAURRANT. *(going up the steps)* Well, I'd better go and start this chicken. Are you coming home for lunch, Rose?

ROSE. Yes. I'll be back, as soon as the funeral's over.

Mrs. Maurrant. Oh, all right. *(as she sees SHIRLEY)* Good morning.

Shirley. *(coming out of the vestibule, reading the post card)* Good morning.

Rose. Good morning. *(MRS. MAURRANT goes into the house.)*

(The shade of MAE'S window flies up and she is seen, for an instant, dressed only in her step-in. She yawns noisily and turns away from the window.)

Rose. *(seating herself on the stoop)* It's another awful day, isn't it?

Shirley. Yes, and when you have to keep forty children quiet—! Well, thank goodness, in two weeks, school closes. Otherwise, I think I'd go crazy.

Rose. Well, you get a nice, long vacation, anyhow.

Shirley. Not much vacation for me. I'm taking summer courses at Teachers' College. *(She looks at ROSE a moment, hesitates, and then comes down the steps.)* Miss Maurrant, if you don't mind, I want to talk to you about my brother, Sam.

Rose. Why certainly, Miss Kaplan.

Shirley. I guess you know he's only finishing college, this month—

Rose. Yes, of course, I do.

Shirley. Then he has to go three years to law school and pass the bar examination, before he can be a full fledged lawyer.

Rose. Yes, it takes a long time.

Shirley. A long time and lots of money. And before a

young lawyer begins to make his own living, that takes a long time, too. It will be ten years, maybe, before he's making enough to support himself and a family. *(looking away)* Then, it's time enough for him to think about marriage.

ROSE. You don't mean me and Sam, Miss Kaplan?

SHIRLEY. Yes, that's just what I mean.

ROSE. Why, we're just good friends, that's all.

SHIRLEY. I know how it is with a boy like Sam, Miss Maurrant. He thinks he's a man, already; but he's nothing but a boy. If you're such a good friend, you shouldn't take his mind away from his work.

ROSE. But I haven't meant to, Miss Kaplan — honest I haven't.

SHIRLEY. I've had to work hard enough to get him as far as he is. And I have my father to take care of, too. The few dollars he makes, writing for the radical papers, don't even pay the rent. Believe me, every dollar I make goes.

ROSE. I know. Sam's often told me how much he owes to you.

SHIRLEY. He doesn't owe me anything. I don't care about the money. Only he should be thinking about his work and not about other things.

ROSE. Yes, he should be thinking about his work. But don't you think there are other things in the world, too, besides just work?

SHIRLEY. Don't you think I know that? I know that just as well as you do. Maybe, you think I'm only an old maid school teacher, without any feelings.

ROSE. Oh, I don't — really I don't!

SHIRLEY. *(turning her head away)* Maybe I'm not a movie vamp, with dimples — but I could have had my chances, too. Only, I wanted to give Sam an education.

ROSE. I haven't tried to vamp Sam, honestly I haven't. We just seemed sort of naturally to like each other.

SHIRLEY. Why must you pick out Sam? You could get other fellows. Anyhow, it's much better to marry with your own kind. When you marry outside your own people, nothing good ever comes of it. You can't mix oil and water.

ROSE. I don't know. I think if people really care about each other—

SHIRLEY. He's nothing but a baby. He sees a pretty face and, right away, he forgets about everything else.

ROSE. *(with a flash of temper)* I know I haven't as much brains as Sam, or as you, either, if that's what you mean.

SHIRLEY. *(contritely, going towards her)* I didn't mean to hurt your feelings. I haven't got anything against you. Only, he's all I've got in the world. What else have I got to live for?

(SAM appears at the extreme right window, with a cup of coffee and a piece of coffee cake.)

SAM. Hello, Rose.

ROSE. Hello, Sam.

SHIRLEY. *(in a low tone)* Please don't tell him what I said. *(SAM goes to the other window.)*

ROSE. Oh no, I won't. *(SHIRLEY hurries off, at the left. ROSE rises and turns toward SAM.)* Sam—

SAM. *(holding out the coffee cake)* Want some coffee cake?

ROSE. No. *(going up the steps)* Sam, there's something I want to ask you, before I forget. Is there any special way you have to act in a synagogue?

SAM. *(eating throughout)* In a synagogue?

ROSE. Yes. The funeral I'm going to, is in a synagogue, and I thought there might be some special thing you have to do. Like in church, you know, a girl is always supposed to keep her hat on.

SAM. I don't know. I've never in my life been in a synagogue.

ROSE. Didn't you ever go to Sunday school, or anything like that?

SAM. No.

ROSE. That's funny. I thought everybody went, once in a while. How about when your mother died?

SAM. She was cremated. My parents were always rationalists.

ROSE. Didn't they believe in God or anything?

SAM. What do you mean by God?

ROSE. *(puzzled)* Well — you know what I mean. What anybody means — God. Somebody that sort of loves us and looks after us, when we're in trouble.

SAM. *(sitting on the window sill)* That's nothing but superstition — the lies that people tell themselves, because reality is too terrible for them to face.

ROSE. But, Sam, don't you think it's better to believe in something that makes you a little happy, than not to believe in anything and be miserable all the time?

SAM. There's no such thing as happiness. That's an

illusion, like all the rest.

ROSE. Then, what's the use of living?

SAM. *(brushing the last crumbs off his hands)* Yes, what is the use?

ROSE. Why, you oughtn't to talk like that, Sam — a person with all the talent and brains that you've got. I know things aren't just the way you want them to be. But they aren't for anybody. They aren't for me, either.

SAM. Then, why don't we get out of it, together?

ROSE. I don't see just how we could do that, Sam.

SAM. It would be easy enough — ten cents worth of carbolic acid.

ROSE. Why, Sam, you don't mean kill ourselves!

SAM. Is your life so precious to you that you want to cling to it?

ROSE. Well, yes. I guess it is.

SAM. Why? Why? What is there in life to compensate for the pain of living?

ROSE. There's a lot. Just being alive — breathing and walking around. Just looking at the faces of people you like and hearing them laugh. And seeing the pretty things in the store windows. And rough housing with your kid brother. And — oh, I don't know — listening to a good band, and dancing — Oh, I'd hate to die! *(earnestly)* Sam, promise you won't talk about killing yourself, any more.

SAM. What difference would it make to you, if I did?

ROSE. Don't talk like that, Sam! You're the best friend I've ever had. *(She puts her hand on his.)*

SAM. I can't think of anything but you.

Rose. There's something I want to ask your advice about, Sam. It's about what I started to tell you about, last night. A man I know wants to put me on the stage.

Sam. *(releasing her hand and drawing back)* What man?

Rose. A man that works in the office. He knows a manager and he says he'll help me get started. You see, what I thought was, that if I could only get out of here and have a decent place to live and make a lot of money, maybe everything would be different, not only for me, but for ma and pop and Willie.

Sam. But don't you know what he wants, this man?

Rose. Nobody gives you anything for nothing, Sam. If you don't pay for things in one way, you do in another.

Sam. Rose, for God's sake, you mustn't!

(VINCENT JONES comes out of the house.)

Rose. *(seeing VINCENT in the vestibule)* Look out, Sam, here's that tough, from upstairs. *(She goes over to the left of the stoop.)*

Vincent. *(in the doorway)* Hello, Rosie. Been here, all night, talkin' to the little yit? *(ROSE does not answer.)*

Vincent. *(turning to SAM)* Hello, motzers! Shake! *(He leans over the balustrade and seizes SAM'S hand, in a crushing grip.)*

Sam. *(writhing with pain)* Let me go!

Rose. Let him alone! *(VINCENT gives SAM'S hand another vicious squeeze and then releases him. SAM cowers back in the window, nursing his hand.)*

Vincent. *(waving his hand about in mock pain)* Jesus, what

a grip dat little kike's got! I'd hate to get into a mix-up wit'
him. *(to ROSE:)* Got a date for to-night, kid?

ROSE. Yes, I have.

VINCENT. Yeah? Gee, ain't dat too bad. I'll give you two
dollars, if you let me snap your garter.

ROSE. Shut up, you! *(VINCENT laughs. SAM makes an
inarticulate sound.)*

VINCENT. *(threateningly)* Whadja say? I t'ought I hoid
you say sumpin. *(He makes a threatening gesture. SAM
shrinks back.)*

VINCENT. *(with a loud laugh, as he goes down the steps)*
Fightin' Kaplan, de pride o' Jerusalem! *(He looks at them
both, then laughs again.)* Fer cryin' out loud! *(He goes off
at the left.)*

ROSE. Oh, if there was only some way of getting out of
here! *(SAM puts the back of his hand to his forehead and turns
away.)* I sometimes think I'd just like to run away.

SAM. *(without turning)* Yes!

ROSE. Anywhere — it wouldn't matter where — just to
get out of this.

SAM. *(turning)* Why shouldn't we do it?

ROSE. *(rather startled coming over to the right balustrade)*
Would you go with me, Sam?

SAM. Yes — anywhere.

ROSE. I've heard that people are much nicer and
friendlier, when you get outside of New York. There's not
so much of a mad rush, other places. And being alone,
you could sort of work things out for yourself. *(suddenly)*
Only what would you do, Sam?

SAM. I could get a job, too.

ROSE. And give up your law work?

SAM. I'd give up everything, to be with you.

ROSE. No. I wouldn't let you do that, Sam. it's different with me—

(EASTER appears at the right.)

EASTER. *(stopping at the right of the stoop)* Good morning, Miss Maurrant. *(startled, ROSE turns and sees him, for the first time)*

ROSE. *(none too pleased)* Oh, good morning, Mr. Easter. What brings you in this neighborhood?

EASTER. *(not very plausibly)* Well, I just happened to have a little business, right around the corner. So, I thought as long as you were going to the funeral, we might just as well go together.

ROSE. Well, I hardly expected to see you around here. *(an awkward pause)* Oh, I'd like you to meet my friend, Mr. Kaplan.

EASTER. How do you do, Mr. Kaplan? Glad to know you. *(SAM murmurs something inaudible. An awkward silence.)*

ROSE. *(to SAM:)* Mr. Easter is the manager of the office. *(SAM does not reply. Another silence. To EASTER:)* It's awful hot again, isn't it?

EASTER. Worse than yesterday. *(approaching the stoop)* Tell you what I was thinking. I was thinking, that after the funeral, we might take a run down to the beach, somewhere, and cool off a little.

ROSE. I can't today. I've got a lot of things I want to do.

EASTER. Oh, you can do 'em some other day.

Rose. No, really, I can't. *(looking at her watch)* Well, I guess it's time we got started. *(She comes down the steps.)*

Easter. Yes, it is. We'll pick up a cab at the corner.

(MRS. MAURRANT appears at her window, looks out, and sees ROSE and EASTER.)

Rose. Why, I thought I'd walk. It's not far.

Easter. Too hot, today, for any walking.

Rose. *(starting to go towards the left)* Not if you keep in the shade.

Easter. Much more comfortable taking a cab.

Rose. I'd rather walk.

Easter. Well, whatever you say. Good morning, Mr. Kaplan. Glad to have met you. *(SAM murmurs an inaudible reply.)*

Rose. Good-bye, Sam. I'll see you later. *(SAM does not answer. ROSE and EASTER go towards the left, in silence. SAM watches them, intently, trembling with jealousy. MRS. MAURRANT, surprised and disturbed, watches ROSE and EASTER.)*

Rose. *(to EASTER: as they disappear)* It's a lucky thing my father wasn't around. *(SAM suddenly turns and goes into the house. MRS. MAURRANT remains at the window, looking out, with obvious expectancy.)*

A Distant Voice. *(offstage)* Straw-berries! Strawberries!

(An anemic girl of eighteen, with a music roll under her arm, appears at the left. She Enters the house and pushes one of the buttons, in the vestibule, then goes to the entrance door and waits. A

moment later, MRS. FIORENTINO appears hastily, at the window, and whisks away the bed clothes. After another moment, the latch clicks and the girl Enters the house.)

THE VOICE. *(a little nearer) Oh-h! Straw-*berries! Strawberries!

(SANKEY appears at the right. He carries a pencil behind his ear, wears a round cap with a metal name plate and a stiff visor, and carries a large black covered bill holder. He and MRS. MAURRANT see each other and both become tense with excitement. MRS. MAURRANT beckons to him and he comes over to the railing, under her window.)

MRS. MAURRANT. *(in a love, tense voice)* Come up.
SANKEY. *(looking about, nervously)* Now?
MRS. MAURRANT. Yes. I got to talk to you.
SANKEY. Is it all right?
MRS. MAURRANT. Yes. He's gone to Stamford.
SANKEY. How about later?
MRS. MAURRANT. No. Rose'll be home in a hour. She's not working today.
SANKEY. All right. *(He looks about again, then goes quickly towards the steps.)*

(SAM appears, at the entrance door. He is about to step out, when he sees SANKEY. He stops and looks at him. SANKEY sees SAM, hesitates a moment, then goes quickly into the houe. Meanwhile, MRS. MAURRANT has closed both windows and pulled down the shades. SAM takes a periodical out of the mailbox, then comes out of the house and down the steps. He looks up at the MAURRANT

windows, sees the drawn shades, and looks about, in perturbed per-
plexity, not knowing what to do. At length, he sits down on the steps
of the stoop, tears the wrapper off the periodical — The Nation —
and begins to read. The girl in LIPPO'S apartment begins playing
the piano. This continues throughout the scene. Two untidy and
rather coarse looking men appear, at the left and approach the
stoop: JAMES HENRY, a city marshal, and FRED CULLEN, his
assistant. They stop in front of the house. SAM pays no
attention to them.)

THE MARSHAL. *(crossing to the left of the stoop, and taking a*
paper from his pocket) Dis is it. *(to SAM:)* Hildebrand live
here?

SAM. *(startled)* What?

THE MARSHAL. I'm askin' you if Hildebrand lives
here.

SAM. Yes. Fourth floor.

THE MARSHAL. Better give de janitor a buzz, Fred.
(FRED goes up the steps and rings the janitor's bell, then leans over
the left balustrade.)

FRED. *(bawling)* Hey, janitor.

OLSEN. *(below)* Vell?

FRED. Come on out, a minute.

(FRED speaks as OLSEN appears below.)

FRED. We got a warrant for Hildebrand.

OLSEN. Fourt' floor — Hildebrand.

FRED. Yeah, I know. We got a warrant for her.

THE MARSHAL. I'm City Marshal Henry. We got a dis-
possess warrant.

OLSEN. *(coming up the steps)* Oh, sure. You gonna put 'em out?

THE MARSHAL. Yeah, dat's it. Has she got anybody to take de foinicher away?

OLSEN. *(with a shrug)* I don' know.

THE MARSHAL. Well, we'll have t' dump it on de sidewalk, den. Go ahead, Fred.

(They Enter the house. OLSEN leans his elbows on the coping, and smokes his pipe. SAM sits on the steps, deep in troubled thought. A grocery boy, with a full basket, appears at the right, and goes down the cellar steps. MAE JONES comes out of the house. She stands on the top step, yawns noisily, and goes off, at left. She and SAM do not pay the slightest attention to each other.)

A VOICE. *(a little nearer)* Straw-berries! Straw-*berries!*

(MRS. OLSEN comes up the cellar steps, with a heavy pail of water. OLSEN leans forward to make room for her. She staggers over to the stoop, almost dropping the pail, and goes up the steps, into the vestibule. OLSEN yawns and goes down into the cellar. MRS. JONES appears, at the window, her hair wet and stringy, a towel pinned about her shoulders, and leans out to dry her hair. An OLD-CLOTHES MAN appears at the left.)

AN OLD-CLOTHES MAN. I kesh ko! I kesh ko! *(He wears a battered derby and carries a folded newspaper under his arm. MRS. OLSEN, on her knees, begins washing up the vestibule. FRED comes out of the house, carrying a worn chair and a large gilt-framed picture, which he deposits on the sidewalk, against the railing, to the left of the stoop. The OLD-CLOTHES MAN speaks as if to someone across the street.)* Kesh ko? *(to SAM:)* Any old

klose, mister? (SAM pays no attention to him. FRED re-enters
the house. To MRS. JONES:) Any ol' klose, leddy?

    MRS. JONES. Naw, nawthin'.

    AN OLD-CLOTHES MAN. Hets? Shoes? Ol' stockings?

    MRS. JONES. Nawthin', I tell you.

(As the OLD-CLOTHES MAN goes off, at the right. MAUR-
RANT appears, still carrying his satchel.)

    MRS. JONES. Why, hello, Mr. Maurrant. (MAURRANT
looks up without replying and comes over to the stoop.) I thought
you was off to Stamford.

    MAURRANT. I changed me — (He stops, to the right of the
stoop, and looks up at the drawn shades of his apartment. SAM
rises, slowly and rigidly, his eyes glued in fascination, upon
MAURRANT. MAURRANT'S movements take on a lithe and cat
like quality. Then, slowly and deliberately, he goes towards the
steps, his back arched, like a tiger ready to spring.)

    SAM. (suddenly blocking the steps) No! No! For God's
sake—!

    MAURRANT. (raging) Out o' me way, you goddam little
rat! (He flings SAM violently aside, almost knocking him down.
MRS. OLSEN, terrified, rises, and shrinks into a corner, as
MAURRANT with swift stealthiness, Enters the house. MRS.
JONES leans out, to see what is wrong. SAM rushes down the
steps and stands under the MAURRANT windows. The
MARSHAL comes out of the house, carrying a wash boiler, filled
with pots.)

    SAM. (hysterically) Mrs. Maurrant! Mrs. Maurrant!

    MRS. JONES. What's the matter? (The MARSHAL puts the
wash boiler on the balustrade and looks on in amazement.)

SAM. *(to MRS. JONES:)* Quick! Run and tell her! Quick!

MRS. JONES. What is it? *(suddenly)* Oh, Gawd, is he in there? *(She leaves the window, hastily.)*

SAM. Yes! Mrs. Maurrant! Mrs. Maurrant!

(A scream of terror is heard, from the MAURRANT apartment.)

MRS. MAURRANT'S VOICE. Frank! Frank!

(Two shots are heard, in quick succession, and then a heavy fall. MRS. OLSEN runs out of the vestibule and down into the cellar. SANKEY's voice is heard, inarticulate with fear. Then, one of the shades shoots up, and SANKEY appears at the window, coatless, his face deformed by terror. He tries to open the window, but succeeds only in shattering the pane with his elbow. MAURRANT appears behind him and pulls him away from the window. Then another shot is heard.)

THE MARSHAL. For Chris' sake, what's happenin'? Get an ambulance, you!

(He pushes SAM towards the left, then hurries off, at the right. As SAM runs off, a crowd begins to form. OLSEN comes up from the cellar, followed by the GROCERY-BOY. The two workmen come up, out of the excavation. Two or three of the workmen from the demolished building, run on at the right.)

THE WORKMAN. What's happening?

A MAN. What is it? A murder?

(Still others join the crowd: A huckster, a janitor from a neighboring house, a mulatto girl, six or eight women of the neighborhood, some in street dresses, others in house dresses or dingy wrappers. LIP-PO'S pupil appears, at the window, badly frightened. The crowd surges about, uncertainly, not knowing what has happened, and buzzing with questions, which nobody can answer. While the crowd is still forming, FRED, the MARSHAL'S assistant, appears at the broken window.)

FRED. *(excitedly)* Grab dat boid! He's comin' down!
THE WORKMAN. What boid?
A MAN. Here he is, now!

(The crowd murmurs with excitement and surges about the stoop, as the house door opens and MAURRANT appears. His coat is open and his shirt is torn almost to shreds. His face, hands and clothing are covered with blood. He stands, in the doorway, for a moment, surveying the crowd, his eyes glaring.)

FRED. Grab him! Don't let him get away! *(As the crowd makes a concerted movement towards MAURRANT, he whips out an automatic revolver and levels it. The crowd shrinks back. Some of the women scream.)*
MAURRANT. Git back! Git back, all o' you! *(The crowd falls back towards the left, to make way for him. With his back to the balustrade, he comes quickly down the steps, and still leveling his revolver at the crowd, retreats backwards to the cellar steps.)*

(A man, approaching at the right, comes stealthily up behind him, but MAURRANT senses his presence in time, wheels quickly menaces the man with his revolver, then rushes down the cellar

steps. While all this is happening, the other shade in the
MAURRANT apartment flies up and MISS CUSHING opens the
window and leans out.)

MISS CUSHING. Hurry up! Get an ambulance! *(No one*
pays any attention to her, as they are all watching MAURRANT.
As MAURRANT runs down the cellar steps, the crowd surges for-
ward to the railing, on both sides of the stoop and leans over.)

(A scream from MRS. OLSEN is heard from the basement. FRED
goes away from the window.)

MISS CUSHING. Get an ambulance, somebody! *(Unable*
to attract anyone's attention, she leaves the window.)

OLSEN. Olga! *(He hurries down the cellar steps.)*
A MAN. *(calling)* Here's a cop! *(The crowd looks to the*
right.) Hey! Hurry up!

(A POLICEMAN runs on from the right.)

THE POLICEMAN. Where is he?
VOICES IN THE CROWD. He's down the cellar! He ran
down the cellar! He went down the steps!
THE POLICEMAN. Get out of the way! *(The POLICEMAN*
and two men in the crowd go down the cellar steps.)
VOICES IN THE CROWD. Watch yourself! Look out, he's
got a gun! He's a big guy with his shirt torn! *(The rest of the*
crowd peers over the railing.)
MISS CUSHING. *(leaning out of ROSE'S window)* Hey,
don't you hear me? Get an ambulance!

ANOTHER MAN. *(looking up)* What's de matter? You want de ambulance?

MISS CUSHING. Yes! Right away!

ANOTHER MAN. *(to the GROCERY-BOY.)* Run around' de corner to de horspital, Johnny, an' tell 'em to send de ambulance!

THE GROCERY-BOY. Sure!

MISS CUSHING. Run! *(The GROCERY-BOY runs off swiftly at the left. MISS CUSHING leaves the window. Meanwhile, as the POLICEMAN and the TWO MEN have gone down the cellar steps, the MARSHAL has run on, from the right, panting.)*

THE MARSHAL. *(as the GROCERY-BOY runs off)* Did dey git 'em?

A MAN. He beat it down de cellar.

THE WORKMAN. De cop's gone after him.

THE MARSHAL. Why de hell didn' you stop 'im?

(FRED comes out of the house.)

THE WORKMAN. He had a gun.

FRED. Did somebody go for de ambulance?

A MAN. Yeah. De kid went.

A WOMAN. It's only aroun' de corner.

ANOTHER MAN. Dey'll be here, right away. *(The crowd moves over towards FRED.)*

THE MARSHAL. *(pushing his way through the crowd and up the steps)* What de hell happened, Fred?

FRED. *(as the crowd moves toward the stoop)* It's a moider. Dis boid's wife an' some other guy. Jesus, you oughta see de blood.

(Another POLICEMAN runs up, at the left, closely followed by SAM.)

FRED. Upstairs, officer! Dere's two of 'em got shot.

THE POLICEMAN. *(elbowing his way through the crowd)* Look out o' de way, youse! *(He goes up the stoop and crosses to the door.)* Where's de guy dat did it?

VOICES IN THE CROWD. Down de cellar! He beat it down the steps!

FRED. Dere's another cop after 'im. You better look after dem, upstairs. Foist floor.

SAM. *(agonized)* Are they dead? *(No one pays any attention to him.)*

THE MARSHAL. *(stopping the POLICEMAN, and exhibiting his badge)* I'm City Marshal Henry. Kin I do anythin'?

THE POLICEMAN. Don' let anybody in or out! Hear?

THE MARSHAL. Yeah, sure! *(The POLICEMAN Exits quickly, into the house.)*

SAM. Are they dead? *(No one notices him. The MARSHAL takes up his position in the doorway.)*

(BUCHANAN appears at the MAURRANT window.)

BUCHANAN. Where's the ambulance?

THE MARSHAL. It'll be here, right away. Dere's a cop on his way up.

SAM. Mr. Buchanan! Mr. Buchanan! Are they dead? *(But BUCHANAN has already disappeared. The TWO MEN, who followed the first POLICEMAN into the cellar, now come up the steps. The crowd moves over to the railing, at the right.)*

THE MARSHAL. Did you get him, boys?

ONE OF THE MEN. He must be hidin', somewheres. De cop's lookin' for 'im.

ANOTHER MAN. Somebody better call de resoives. *(SAM runs up the steps and tries to Enter the house.)*

THE MARSHAL. *(seizing him roughly)* You can't get in now! Get back dere! *(He pushes SAM back into the crowd, at the foot of the steps.)*

(The POLICEMAN at the MAURRANT window.)

THE POLICEMAN. Hey, call up headquarters an' tell 'em to send the resoives. Make it quick! *(He goes away from the window.)*

THE MARSHAL. You go, Fred.

FRED. Sure!

A MAN. Dere's a phone in de warehouse.

(An ambulance bell is heard at the left, as FRED goes quickly towards the left. Another spectator hurries on and joins the crowd.)

VOICES IN THE CROWD. Dere it is! Dere's de ambulance now! Here dey come! *(The crowd moves over towards the left.)*

A MAN. Dey won't be able to git past.

THE POLICEMAN. *(reappearing at the window)* Is dat de ambulance?

THE MARSHAL. Yeah.

(BUCHANAN and MRS. JONES crowd to the window, behind the POLICEMAN, and at the other window, LIPPO, MISS

CUSHING and MRS. HILDEBRAND appear. A hospital interne and an ambulance driver come on at the left.)

THE POLICEMAN. Hurry up, Doc! She's still breathin'.

THE INTERNE. *(forcing his way through the crowd)* All right! Better bring the stretcher, Harry.

THE AMBULANCE-DRIVER. Yes, sir. *(He hurries off, at the left. The INTERNE goes quickly into the house. The crowd attempts to follow, several of its members going up the steps.)*

THE MARSHAL. *(pushing them back)* Keep back, now! Back off de stoop, everybody!

(The crowd forms a compact mass, about the foot of the steps. The persons at the MAURRANT windows have disappeared. FRED hurries on, at the left.)

FRED. *(pushing his way through the crowd and up the steps)* I got 'em. Dey'll be right up. Anudder cop jes' wen' in t'roo de warehouse cellar.

THE MARSHAL. Dey'll git 'im all right. *(looking at his watch)* Better git busy wit' dat foinicher, Fred. We got two udder jobs today.

FRED. Yeah, sure, Jimmy. *(He Enters the house.)*

(The AMBULANCE-DRIVER appears at the left, carrying a canvas stretcher.)

THE AMBULANCE-DRIVER. Get out o' the way!

THE MARSHAL. Git back, can't youse? What de hell's de matter wit' youse? *(He comes down the steps and violently pushes the crowd back. The AMBULANCE-DRIVER Enters the house.)*

THE POLICEMAN. *(at the window)* Are dey bringin' dat stretcher?

THE MARSHAL. On de way up! *(to the crowd:)* Keep back! *(The POLICEMAN leaves the window.)*

(LIPPO'S PUPIL, her music roll under her arm, appears timidly in the doorway.)

THE MARSHAL. *(grabbing her arm roughly)* Where you goin'?

THE GIRL. *(nervously)* I'm going home.

THE MARSHAL. Home? Where do you live?

THE GIRL. Ninety-first Street.

THE MARSHAL. What are you doin' here?

THE GIRL. I just came for a music lesson, that's all.

THE MARSHAL. Yeah? Well, you can't go now.

THE GIRL. *(beginning to whimper)* I want to go home.

THE MARSHAL. You can't go, now. Nobody can't leave de house, now.

THE POLICEMAN. *(coming out of the house)* Who's dis kid?

THE MARSHAL. Says she come here to take a music lesson an' she wants to go home.

THE POLICEMAN. *(to the girl:)* Do you know anythin' about this killin'?

THE GIRL. No, I don't. I just heard some shooting, that's all. My mother will be worried, if I don't come home.

THE POLICEMAN. Well, you can't go, now. Get inside dere, out o' de way. Dey'll be bringin' her down, in a minute. *(He pushes the girl inside the house and comes down the steps.)*

THE POLICEMAN. Come on, git back from dem steps! Back now, all o' youse! *(He and the MARSHAL push the crowd back to the right of the stoop, leaving the steps and the sidewalk in front of them clear. Then he goes up the steps again.)*

THE MARSHAL. What did he do? Shoot two of 'em?

THE POLICEMAN. I'll say he did! His wife an' her sweetie. A guy named Sankey. He was dead when I got up dere.

THE MARSHAL. I seen him tryin' to climb out t'roo de winder. An' dis guy grabs 'im an' pulls 'im back.

THE INTERNE. *(from the MAURRANT window)* Officer! Come on up! *(He leaves the window, as the POLICEMAN Exits into the house. Suddenly, SAM utters an exclamation of anguish and, pushing his way out of the crowd, hurries over to the left.)*

THE MARSHAL. Hey, you! Where you goin'? *(SAM ignores him and hurries on.)*

A WOMAN. Look! There's the Maurrant girl!

ANOTHER WOMAN. Who?

A WOMAN. It's her daughter.

(The crowd murmurs, excitedly, as ROSE comes on quickly, at the left.)

ROSE. What's the matter, Sam? What's the ambulance for? Did anybody get hurt?

SAM. Go away, Rose. Go away.

ROSE. Who is it, Sam? What's the matter? Is it my mother? It's not my mother, is it? *(clinging to him)* Sam, is it?

SAM. There's been an accident. Go away, Rose. *(He tries to force her away.)*

ROSE. Tell me what's happened! Tell me!

(MISS CUSHING appears at the window.)

MISS CUSHING. They're bringing her down!

ROSE. *(with a cry)* It *is* my mother!

MISS CUSHING. *(seeing her)* Oh, my God, there's Rose!

(MRS. FIORENTINO, MRS. JONES, MRS. HILDEBRAND, LIPPO and BUCHANAN crowd to the MAURRANT windows.)

SAM. Rose! Go away! *(She pays no attention to him, but stands watching the door, transfixed.)*

(The INTERNE comes briskly out of the house.)

THE INTERNE. *(to the MARSHAL:)* Hold the door open, will you? *(He comes down the steps.)*

THE MARSHAL. Sure, doc! *(He hurries into the vestibule.)*

THE INTERNE. *(to the crowd:)* Keep back, now!

ROSE. *(seizing the INTERNE'S arm)* Doctor! Is she dead?

THE INTERNE. Who are you? Her daughter?

ROSE. Yes, sir. I'm her daughter.

THE INTERNE. She's pretty badly hurt. Step aside, now!

(They step aside, as the AMBULANCE-DRIVER and the POLICEMAN come out of the house, carrying MRS. MAURRANT on the stretcher. There is a low murmur from the crowd.)

THE AMBULANCE-DRIVER. Easy, now.

THE POLICEMAN. All right. *(They come down the steps and go towards the left.)*

ROSE. *(running forward and gripping the side of the stretcher)* Mother! Mother!

MRS. MAURRANT. *(opening her eyes, feebly)* Rose! *(She tries to lift her hand, but it falls back.)*

THE INTERNE. *(pulling ROSE back)* You mustn't talk to her, now. *(SAM takes her about the shoulders. They and the INTERNE follow the stretcher off, at the left. The crowd swarms after them.)*

(FRED comes out of the house, carrying one end of an iron bedstead.)

(CURTAIN)

ACT THREE

Mid-afternoon of the same day. At the left of the stoop, is a large roll of bedding. Before the rise of the curtain, and continuing faintly thereafter, a woman can be heard singing scales. OLSEN, pipe in mouth, is leaning against the railing. two MEN, furniture movers appear at the left.

ONE OF THE MEN. *(picking up the bedding)* All right. Dat's all, Charlie! *(The MEN Exit left.)*

(A POLICEMAN comes out of the house, carrying the blood-stained dress of MRS. MAURRANT, and SANKEY'S coat, cap, and bill-holder. He comes down the steps, and Exits at the right. At the left, Two young NURSE-MAIDS, in smart uniforms, appear, each wheeling a deluxe baby carriage.)

FIRST NURSE-MAID. *(seeing the house number)* This must be the place, right here — 346. *(They stop, under the MAURRANT windows.)*

SECOND NURSE-MAID. Yes, I guess it is.

FIRST NURSE-MAID. Yes, this is it, all right. *(looking up)* Must be right up there, on the first floor, see?

SECOND NURSE-MAID. Yes, sure. *(excitedly)* Say, look! You can see where the glass is out of the window. That's where this feller what's-his-name tried to climb out.

FIRST NURSE-MAID. Oh, yes, I see it! Say, what do you know about that!

SECOND NURSE-MAID. *(taking a pink tabloid newspaper from under the hood of the baby buggy)* Wait! There's a picture of it, somewhere. *(turning the pages)* Here it is. *(They excitedly examine it together, as she read.)* "Composograph showing Sankey, scantily clad, in a last vain attempt to escape the vengeance of the jealousy crazed husband, whose home he had destroyed." And there's Maurrant pulling him back. And Mrs. Maurrant trying to get the pistol away from him, see? Look at the blood running down her face, will you?

FIRST NURSE-MAID. It's worse than awful! Can you *imagine* what those two must have felt like, when he walked in on them like that?

SECOND NURSE-MAID. Well, he just happened to be one of the ones that finds out! Believe me, there's lots and lots of husbands that don't know the half of what goes on up town, while they're down town making a living.

FIRST NURSE-MAID. Say, you're not telling me, are you? If I was to spill all I know, there'd be many a happy home busted up. I wonder if they caught him.

(The baby begins a thin wailing.)

SECOND NURSE-MAID. Oh, God, he's in again! *(to the unseen baby:)* Shut up, a little while, can't you? *(She shakes the carriage.)*

(A POLICEMAN appears at the MAURRANT windows, a tabloid in his hand.)

POLICEMAN. Keep movin', ladies. No loiterin' aroun' here.

FIRST NURSE-MAID. *(eagerly)* Say, have they caught him, yet?

POLICEMAN. Why, ain't you hoid? He was last seen, flyin' over Nova Scotia, on his way to Paris.

FIRST NURSE-MAID. Who are you trying to string, anyhow?

SECOND NURSE-MAID. *(coquettishly)* Say, will you let us come up and look around?

POLICEMAN. Why, sure, sure! Bring de babies, too. De commissioner is soivin' tea, up here, at four-thoity.

SECOND NURSE-MAID. You're awful smart, aren't you?

POLICEMAN. Yeah, dat's why dey put me on de entertainment committee. I'm Handsome Harry Moiphy, de boy comedian o' Brooklyn.

FIRST NURSE-MAID. *(looking at her watch)* Oh, say, I ought to be getting back. *(turning her carriage)* Clarice darling would throw a duck-fit, if she knew I brought her precious Dumplings to a neighborhood like this.

SECOND NURSE-MAID. *(turning her carriage)* There's not so much to see, anyhow. It's nothing but a cheap, common dump. *(They go towards the left.)*

POLICEMAN. Over de river, goils. See you in de funny paper.

SECOND NURSE-MAID. Don't you get so fresh.

POLICEMAN. Drop in again, when you're in de neighborhood. An' tell Mrs. Vanderbilt, Harry was askin' for her.

(As the NURSE-MAIDS go off, at the left, EASTER hurries on at the right, several folded newspapers under his arm.)

EASTER. *(to the POLICEMAN: going to the left of the stoop)* Is Miss Maurrant up there, officer?

POLICEMAN. No. There ain't nobody up here but me.

EASTER. You don't happen to know where she is, do you?

POLICEMAN. No, I don't. Are you a reporter?

EASTER. Who, me? I'm just a friend of hers. I've got to see her.

POLICEMAN. Well, I ain't seen her since she went off to the horspital this mornin'. She ain't been back since. *(He starts to leave the window.)*

EASTER. Oh, officer!

POLICEMAN. Yeah?

EASTER. Have they caught him, yet?

POLICEMAN. Naw, not yet. But we'll get 'im, all right. *(He leaves the window. EASTER remains at the left of the stoop, uncertain whether to go or not.)*

(MRS. JONES appears, at the right, carrying several newspapers.)

MRS. JONES. *(to OLSEN:)* Have they caught him yet?

OLSEN. *(shaking his head)* No.

MRS. JONES. I been down at Police Headquarters, all this while — *(breaking off, as she notices EASTER)* Say, what's he want here? *(OLSEN shrugs his shoulders.)*

EASTER. *(approaching them)* Pardon me, but maybe you can tell me where I can find Miss Maurrant? *(OLSEN shakes his head.)*

MRS. JONES. Why no, I can't. I jus' this minute got back

from Police Headquarters. Maybe she's aroun' at the horspital.

EASTER. No, I just came from there.

MRS. JONES. Well, I really couldn't say where she is. Was there somethin' special you wanted to see her about?

EASTER. I'm a friend of hers—

MRS. JONES. Yeah, I noticed you talkin' to her, last night, when I took the dog out. *(staring at him)* Well, I guess she'll need all the friends she's got, now. Imagine a thing like that happenin' right here in this house, at ten o'clock in the mornin'! Everythin' goin' on just as usual, and then, all of a sudden, before you know it, there's two people murdered.

OLSEN. I tal everybody some day he kill her.

MRS. JONES. Well, I ain't sayin' it's right to kill anybody, but if anybody had a reason, he certainly had. You oughta heard some o' the questions they was askin' me down at the Police. I could feel myself gettin' redder an' redder. "Say," I says, "how do you expect me to know things like that?" *(suddenly, as she looks left)* Here's Rose now!

EASTER. Where? *(He turns quickly and hurries to the left.)*

(ROSE appears, carrying four or five packages.)

MRS. JONES. *(to OLSEN:)* He seems to take a pretty friendly interest in her. *(OLSEN nods.)*

ROSE. *(anxiously, as she comes up to EASTER, at the left of the stoop)* Have they caught him yet?

EASTER. Why no, they haven't. I just asked the officer, upstairs.

ROSE. Oh, I hope he got away! If they get him, there's no telling what they'll do to him. And what would be the good of that? He never would have done it, if he'd been in his right mind.

EASTER. I only heard about it, a little while ago. So I went right around to the hospital. But they said you'd left.

ROSE. *(going to the steps)* She never opened her eyes again. They did everything they could for her, but it didn't help.

EASTER. Here, let me take your bundles.

ROSE. No, it's all right. I think I'll just sit down for a minute. *(She sits on the stoop and puts the packages beside her.)*

EASTER. Can't I get you something? A drink or something?

ROSE. No, I'm all right. It's so hot. *(She puts her hand to her head.)* And all those people asking me a lot of questions.

MRS. JONES. *(approaching the stoop)* Are you feelin' dizzy or anythin'?

ROSE. No, I'll be all right in a minute.

MRS. JONES. Well, I was gonna say, if you want to go up to my flat an' lay down for a minute—

ROSE. No, thanks; I don't want to lie down. I've got to go upstairs to get some things.

EASTER. Why, say, you don't want to go up there!

ROSE. I've got to; there's some things I need.

EASTER. Well, let me get them for you. Or this lady here.

MRS. JONES. Yeah, sure. The place is a sight, up there. You're li'ble to go into a faint or somethin'.

ROSE. I guess nothing can be any worse than what's happened already. *(indicating the bundles)* I got to change my dress. I bought a white dress for her. And white silk stockings. I want her to look pretty.

MRS. JONES. Yeah, white is the nicest.

ROSE. She looks so quiet and natural. You'd think she was asleep.

MRS. JONES. It was the same way with my mother. You'd of thought she was gonna get up, the next minute. *(starting to go up the steps)* Well, I gotta go up an' get me some lunch. Between everythin' happenin' an' goin' down to Police Headquarters an' all, I ain't had a bite to eat since breakfast. *(stopping on the top step, and looking from ROSE to EASTER.)* Well, you certainly never know, when you get up in the mornin', what the day is gonna bring. *(She Enters the house.)*

ROSE. *(rising)* Well, I'd better be going up, too. There's a lot of things to attend to.

EASTER. You better let me come up with you.

ROSE. Why thanks, Mr. Easter. But I'd rather go alone, if you don't mind.

EASTER. But, listen here — you can't go through all this alone — a kid like you. That's why I came around. I knew you'd be needing a helping hand.

ROSE. That's awfully nice of you, Mr. Easter. But I don't need any help, honest I don't. *(She opens one of the packages.)*

EASTER. Why, you can't handle everything yourself! What about a place to live and all that?

ROSE. *(taking a rosette of black crape out of the package)* Well,
I don't exactly know, yet. I'll have to find some place
where Willie and I can live. I'd like it to be some place
where he wouldn't be running around the streets all the
time. You see, there's nobody but me to look out for
him now.

*(OLSEN crosses to the cellar. MRS. JONES appears at her win-
dow and furtively peeps out, at ROSE and EASTER.)*

ROSE. *(as she sees that OLSEN is about to descend the cellar
steps)* Oh, Mr. Olsen!

OLSEN. *(stopping)* Yes ma'am.

ROSE. Would you mind lending me a hammer and
some tacks? I want to put up this crape.

OLSEN. Yes ma'am; I bring 'em right away. *(He goes into
the cellar. MRS. JONES leaves the window.)*

EASTER. *(insistently)* But why won't you let me help
you out?

ROSE. It's terribly nice of you, Mr. Easter. But I'll be
able to manage alone, really I will. It isn't as if I wasn't
young and strong and able to take care of myself. But as it
is, I'd sort of rather not be under obligations.

EASTER. Why, you wouldn't be under any obligations.
I just mean it in a friendly way, that's all.

ROSE. You've been very nice to me and all that, Mr.
Easter. But — well, I've been sort of thinking things over
— you know, about what we talked about last night and
all. And I honestly don't think I'd care about going on the
stage.

EASTER. Say, you've got me all wrong, Rose! Just forget

all about that, will you? I just want to help you out, that's all. *(taking a step towards her)* I think you're one swell kid, and I want to do something for you. I'm not trying to put anything over on you.

(SHIRLEY appears, at the left, carrying her school bag, from which a newspaper protrudes.)

ROSE. Well, that's nice and friendly of you, Mr. Easter. And if I ever do need any help—

SHIRLEY. *(catching sight of ROSE)* Rose! You poor thing! *(She runs up to ROSE and throws her arms about her.)* It's terrible — terrible!

ROSE. Yes, it is. But I sort of had a feeling, all along, that something terrible was going to happen.

(OLSEN comes up the steps, with a hammer and a box of tacks.)

SHIRLEY. How could he do such a thing! I couldn't believe it when I read it.

ROSE. He was out of his mind, when he did it. Oh, I only hope he got away! *(as OLSEN approaches)* Oh, thanks, Mr. Olsen.

OLSEN. I do it.

ROSE. *(giving him the crape)* Oh, would you, please? Right up there, I think. *(She indicates the left of the doorway.)*

OLSEN. *(going up the steps)* Sure.

ROSE. *(going to EASTER and extending her hand)* Thanks for coming around, Mr. Easter. I don't know when I'll be able to get back to the office.

EASTER. Why, that's all right about that. Only, in the meantime, I wish—

ROSE. If I need any help, I'll let you know. *(with a tone of finality in her voice)* Good-bye.

EASTER. All right; but don't forget. *(He hesitates, then decides to go.)* Well, good-bye. *(He goes off at left.)*

ROSE. I've got to go up and get some things that Willie and I need. Sam went to call for him at school and take him around to my aunt's. You see, I didn't want him coming back here. He's only a little kid, after all.

SHIRLEY. Oh, it's such a terrible thing! I can't believe it yet.

OLSEN. *(holding up the crape)* Dis vay?

ROSE. Yes, like that. *(hesitantly, as she picks up her bundles)* Miss Kaplan, it's sort of silly of me, I guess. But I'm kind of afraid to go up there alone. I wonder if you'd mind coming up with me. *(OLSEN tacks up the crape.)*

SHIRLEY. Anything I can do for you, poor child! *(She and ROSE go up the steps.)*

ROSE. Thanks ever so much. *(to OLSEN:)* Thanks, Mr. Olsen. It's awfully nice of you. *(She and SHIRLEY Enter the house. OLSEN Exits down the cellar steps.)*

(KAPLAN appears, at his window, and seating himself, begins to read a newspaper. An under-sized MAN and a tall WOMAN appear at the right. They are dressed for tennis, and carry tennis rackets.)

A MAN. *(as they cross)* He *would* say that.

A WOMAN. So I just looked at him for a moment,

without saying anything. And then, I said: "My dear boy," I said. "What do you expect anyhow, in this day and age?" I said, "Why even Frankl has to do a black bathroom occasionally." I said.

A MAN. *(as they disappear at the left)* Exactly! And what did he say to that?

(BUCHANAN comes out of the house, and, seeing KAPLAN at the window, stops at the right balustrade.)

BUCHANAN. Well, there's been *some* excitement around here, today.

KAPLAN. *(looking up from his paper)* Dees is a terriible t'ing vich hes heppened.

BUCHANAN. I'll say it is! You know, the way I look at it, he didn't have a right to kill the both of them like that. Of course I'm not saying what she did was right, either.

KAPLAN. How ken ve call ourselves ciwilized, ven ve see thet sax jealousy hes de power to avaken in us de primitive pessions of de sevege?

BUCHANAN. *(rather bewildered by this)* Yes, that's true, too. Of course, you can't expect a man to stand by and see his home broken up. But murdering them, like that, is going a little too far. Well, I got to go and phone the doctor. This thing's given my wife a kind of *re*lapse. She thought a lot of Mrs. Maurrant.

(He goes down the steps, and off at the left, as LIPPO appears, at the right.)

LIPPO. *(stopping in front of KAPLAN's window)* Dey don'

ketcha Maurrant, ha?

KAPLAN. I hevn't hoid anyt'ing foider.

LIPPO. He'sa gonna gat da 'lectrica-chair, ha?

KAPLAN. De bloodlust of our enlightened population must be setisfied! De Chreestian state will kerry out to de last letter de Mosaic law.

LIPPO. Eef Ahm ketcha my wife sleepin' wit' 'nudder man, Ahm gonna keela 'er, too. *(SAM hurries on at the left.)*

KAPLAN. So you t'ink thet merriage should give to de hosband de power of life and det' and thet—

SAM. *(going up the steps)* Papa, is there any news of Maurrant?

KAPLAN. I hev heard notting.

SAM. The police are going to make me testify against him. What can I do, papa?

KAPLAN. You ken do notting.

SAM. How can I send a man to the electric-chair? How can I? I tried to stop him, papa. I tried to warn her—

(He stops short, as several shots are heard offstage, at the left.)

SAM. What's that?

LIPPO. *(excitedly)* Dey finda 'im! *(He runs off, at the left, followed by SAM.)*

(KAPLAN leans out of the window. At the same moment, MRS. JONES leans out of her window and, a moment later, MRS. FIORENTINO out of hers. In the MAURRANT apartment, the POLICEMAN leans out and ROSE and SHIRLEY appear in the hall bedroom window. ROSE is wearing a mourning dress.

OLSEN comes up the cellar steps and runs off at the left. MRS. OLSEN comes up the steps. Several MEN and WOMEN appear at the right and run off at the left.)

ROSE. *(agitatedly)* Is that him?
POLICEMAN. Must be!

(VOICES are heard shouting, in the distance, and then another shot. The POLICEMAN leaves the window.)

ROSE. Oh, God! They wouldn't shoot him, would they? *(She leaves the window.)*
SHIRLEY. *(following her)* Rose!

(Two or three more persons appear at the right and run off at the left. The POLICEMAN runs out of the house, as BUCHANAN appears at the left.)

BUCHANAN. *(excitedly)* They got him! *(The POLICEMAN runs off, at the left.)*

(SHIRLEY reappears at the MAURRANT window.)

MRS. JONES. *(calling)* Have they got him?
BUCHANAN. Yes! He was hiding in the furnace, down at 322. *(as ROSE comes out of the house)* They found him, Miss Maurrant!
ROSE. *(her hand to her heart)* Oh! Is he hurt?
BUCHANAN. I don't know. He fired at the cops and they fired back at him. I was just passing the house, when it happened.

MRS. JONES. *(leaning far out)* Here they come! *(She leaves the window.)*

(The low murmur of the approaching crowd can be heard, offstage left.)

ROSE. Where? *(She comes down the stoop and looks off, at the left.)* Oh! *(She covers her eyes and turns away.)*

MRS. FIORENTINO. You better come inside.

SHIRLEY. Come up, Rose.

BUCHANAN. Yes, you better. *(He takes her by the arm.)*

ROSE. *(resisting)* No. No. Please let me alone. I want to see him. *(She leans against the railing.)*

(The murmur and tramp of the approaching crowd has grown nearer and nearer.)

MRS. FIORENTINO. Look at him, vill you!

(MISS CUSHING comes out of the house, and stands on the stoop, followed a moment later, by MRS. JONES. MAURRANT appears at the left, between two policemen. Behind him a third POLICE-MAN holds back a swarming crowd, which includes SAM and LIPPO. MAURRANT'S clothes are torn, and his right arm is in a crude sling. Sweat, blood and grime have made him almost unrecognizable. The POLICEMEN, too, show evidences of a struggle.)

ROSE. *(running forward)* Pop! Are you hurt?

MAURRANT. *(seeing her for the first time)* Rose!

ONE OF THE POLICEMEN. *(to whom MAURRANT is*

manacled) Keep back, miss!

MAURRANT. It's me daughter! Fer Chris' sake, boys, lemme talk to be daughter! Maybe I'll never be seein' her again!

FIRST POLICEMAN. Give 'im a woid wit' her. *(He is the Officer who was on duty in the MAURRANT apartment.)*

SECOND POLICEMAN. *(after a moment's hesitation)* Well, all right. *(savagely to MAURRANT)* But don't try to pull nothin', hear? *(There is a forward movement in the crowd.)*

FIRST POLICEMAN. *(to the crowd:)* Keep back, youse!

MAURRANT. Rose! You're wearin' a black dress, Rose!

ROSE. Oh, pop, why did you do it? Why did you?

MAURRANT. I must o' been out o' me head, Rose. Did she say anythin'?

ROSE. She never opened her eyes again.

MAURRANT. I'd been drinkin', Rose — see what I mean? — an' all the talk that was goin' around. I just went clean off me nut, that's all.

ROSE. What'll they do to you, pop?

MAURRANT. It's the chair for me, I guess. But I don't care — let 'em give me the chair. I deserve it all right. But it's her, I'm thinkin' of, Rose — the way she looked at me. I oughtn't to done it, Rose.

ROSE. She was always so good and sweet.

MAURRANT. Don't I know it? I ain't no murderer — you ought to be the one to know that, Rose. I just went out o' me head, that's all it was.

SECOND POLICEMAN. All right, that's all now. Come on!

MAURRANT. Gimme a minute, can't you? She's me

daughter. Gimme a chance, can't you? What's gonna happen to you, Rose?

ROSE. I'll be all right, pop. You don't need to worry about me.

MAURRANT. I ain't been a very good father, have I?

ROSE. Don't worry about that, pop.

MAURRANT. It ain't that I ain't meant to be. It's just the way things happened to turn out, that's all. Keep your eye on Willie, Rose. Don't let Willie grow up to be a murderer, like his pop.

ROSE. I'm going to do all I can for him, pop.

MAURRANT. You're a good girl, Rose. You was always a good girl.

ROSE. *(breaking down)* Oh, pop! *(She throws her arms about his neck and buries her head against him. MAURRANT sobs hoarsely.)*

FIRST POLICEMAN. *(gently)* Come on, now, miss. *(He and SAM take ROSE away from MAURRANT.)*

SECOND POLICEMAN. All right. come on, Charlie.

(They go towards the right, the crowd swarming behind them. Straggling along at the very end of the crowd, is an unkempt WOMAN, wheeling a ramshackle baby carriage. MRS. JONES and MISS CUSHING fall in with the crowd. ROSE gradually recovers her self-control, and stands at the stoop, with SAM beside her. The OTHERS watch the receding crowd for a moment. Then KAPLAN and MRS. FIORENTINO leave their windows. The FIRST POLICEMAN Enters the house, followed by LIPPO. MRS. OLSEN goes to the cellar. SHIRLEY looks down at ROSE and SAM, for a moment, then abruptly leaves the window.)

SAM. *(taking ROSE by the arm)* Rose, you better come inside.

ROSE. No, I'm all right again, Sam — honestly I am. *(trying to regain her self-composure)* What about Willie, Sam?

SAM. I told him an accident had happened.

ROSE. It's better to break it to him, that way. But I'll have to tell him, I guess. He'd only find it out himself, tomorrow, with the papers all full of it. I saw Mrs. Sankey, down at Police Headquarters. It's terrible for her, with two little children.

(SHIRLEY appears at the MAURRANT window, a covered pot in her hand.)

SHIRLEY. Rose!

ROSE. *(looking up)* Yes, Miss Kaplan?

SHIRLEY. There's a chicken here, that I found on the gas stove.

ROSE. A chicken?

SHIRLEY. Yes. The policeman says he smelt it cooking, this morning, so he turned out the gas.

ROSE. Oh, I remember, now. My mother said she was going to make some soup for poor Mrs. Buchanan, upstairs.

SHIRLEY. It won't keep long, in this weather.

ROSE. No. I really think Mrs. Buchanan ought to have the good of it.

SHIRLEY. All right. I'll take it up to her.

ROSE. Thanks ever so much, Miss Kaplan. *(Shirley leaves the window.)* It's only a few hours ago that she was standing right here, telling me about the chicken. And then, she went upstairs, and the next I saw of her, they were carrying her out. *(abruptly, as she starts to go up the steps)* Well, I've got to go up and get my things.

SAM. I must talk to you! What are you going to do, Rose?

ROSE. Well, I haven't really had any time to do much thinking. But I really think the best thing I could do, would be to get out of New York. You know, like we were saying, this morning — how things might be different, if you only had a chance to breathe and spread out a little. Only when I said it, I never dreamt it would be this way.

SAM. If you go, I'll go with you.

ROSE. But, Sam dear—

SAM. I don't care anything about my career. It's you — you — I care about. Do you think I can stay here, stifling to death, in this slum, and never seeing you? Do you think my life means anything to me, without you?

ROSE. But, Sam, we've got to be practical about it. How would we manage?

SAM. I don't care what I do. I'll be a day-laborer; I'll dig sewers — anything. *(taking her passionately in his arms)* Rose, don't leave me!

ROSE. I like you so much, Sam. I like you better than anybody I know.

SAM. I love you, Rose. Let me go with you!

ROSE. It would be so nice to be with you. You're different from anybody I know. But I'm just wondering how it would work out.

SAM. If we have each other, that's the vital thing, isn't it? What else matters but that?

ROSE. Lots of things, Sam. There's lots of things to be considered. Suppose something was to happen — well, suppose I was to have a baby, say. That sometimes happens, even when you don't want it to. What would we do, then? We'd be tied down then, for life, just like all the other people around here. They all start out loving each other and thinking that everything is going to be fine — and before you know it, they find out they haven't got anything and they wish they could do it all over again — only it's too late.

SAM. It's to escape all that, that we must be together. It's only because we love each other and belong to each other, that we can find the strength to escape.

ROSE. *(shaking her head)* No, Sam.

SAM. Why do you say no?

ROSE. It's what you said just now — about people belonging to each other. I don't think people ought to belong to anybody but themselves. I was thinking, that if my mother had really belonged to herself, and that if my father had really belonged to himself, it never would have happened. It was only because they were always depending on somebody else, for what they ought to have had inside themselves. Do you see what I mean, Sam? That's why I don't want to belong to anybody, and why I don't want anybody to belong to me.

SAM. You want to go through life alone? — never loving anyone, never having anyone love you?

ROSE. Why, of course not, Sam! I want love more than anything else in the world. But loving and belonging aren't the same thing. *(putting her arms about ·him)* Sam dear, listen. If we say good-bye, now, it doesn't mean that it has to be forever. Maybe some day, when we're older and wiser, things will be different. Don't look as if it was the end of the world, Sam!

SAM. It *is* the end of my world.

ROSE. It isn't, Sam! If you'd only believe in yourself, a little more, things wouldn't look nearly so bad. Because once you're sure of yourself, the things that happen to you, aren't so important. The way I look at it, it's not what you do that matters so much; it's what you are. *(warmly)* I'm so fond of you, Sam. And I've got such a lot of confidence in you. *(impulsively)* Give me a nice kiss! *(SAM takes her in his arms and kisses her, passionately.)*

(A gawky GIRL of seventeen — one of LIPPO'S pupils, appears at the left, and looks at them, scandalized. Then she goes into the vestibule and rings the bell. The door clicks and she Enters the house, as SHIRLEY comes out, carrying a wicker suitcase. SHIRLEY looks at SAM and ROSE.)

ROSE. *(to SHIRLEY:)* I was just telling Sam, that I think I'll soon be going away from New York. *(SAM looks at her, for a moment, in agony, then goes abruptly into the house.)*

SHIRLEY. I put your things in this suitcase. *(She comes down to the pavement. The GIRL, in the FIORENTINO apartment, begins tuning her violin.)*

ROSE. *(taking the suitcase)* You've been awfully nice to me. Don't worry about Sam, Miss Kaplan. Everything will be all right with him.

SHIRLEY. I hope so.

(From the FIORENTINO apartment, come the strains of

Dvořák's Humoresque, jerkily played on a violin.)

ROSE. Oh, I just know it will! *(extending her hand)* Good-bye, Miss Kaplan.

SHIRLEY. Good-bye, Rose. *(impulsively)* You're a sweet girl! *(She hugs and kisses her.)*

ROSE. I hope I'll see you, again.

SHIRLEY. *(crying)* I hope so, Rose. *(ROSE takes up the suitcase and goes off at the left. SHIRLEY stands watching her.)*

(KAPLAN re-appears at his window.)

KAPLAN. Shoiley, vot's de metter again vit Sem? He's crying on de bed.

SHIRLEY. Let him alone, papa, can't you. *(She turns and Enters the house. KAPLAN sighs and, seating himself at the window, opens a newspaper.)*

(A shabby, middle aged couple appear at the right and approach the stoop.)

THE MAN. *(reading the To-Let sign)* Here's a place. Six rooms. Want to take a look at it?

(A group of children offstage left, begins singing The Farmer in the Dell. This continues until after the curtain is down.)

THE WOMAN. All right. No harm lookin'. Ring for the janitor. *(The MAN goes up the stoop and rings the janitor's bell.)* Somebody must o' just died.

THE MAN. Yeah, maybe that's why they're movin' out.

(wiping his face with a handkerchief) Phoo! Seems to be gettin' hotter every minute.

(MRS. FIORENTINO seats herself, at her window, a sewing basket in her lap. MRS. JONES and MISS CUSHING appear at the right, busily engaged in conversation.)

MISS CUSHING. The poor little thing!

MRS. JONES. *(as they go up the steps)* Well, you never can tell with them quiet ones. It wouldn't surprise me a bit, if she turned out the same way as her mother. She's got a gentleman friend, that I guess ain't hangin' around for nothin'. I seen him, late last night, and this afternoon, when I come home from the police — *(She is still talking, as they Enter the house.)*

(MRS. OLSEN comes up the cellar steps. A SAILOR appears at the left, with two girls, an arm about the waist of each. They stroll slowly across.)

The curtain falls.

THE END